Hard-Circus Road

Hard-Circus Road
The Odyssey of the
North Carolina Symphony

BENJAMIN SWALIN

The North Carolina Symphony Society, Inc.

RALEIGH

Contents

Contents

Appendixes

Foreword

Hard-Circus Road is an engaging, delightful account that had to be told for the good of all North Carolinians because it is the story of a North Carolina triumph. But it is also a story of American triumph, of another chapter in the civilization of America, the adornment of the arts and the understanding of the arts.

This is much more than the account of an orchestra. It is a wonderful story of human persistence, of the growth of an idea to glorious fulfillment, of overcoming travail while bowling over barriers, and of keeping a relentless march to the chosen excellence. The young minds that ponder this story might well catch the inspiration of what one good individual idea can become with dedication and drive and vision.

In the years of the Great Depression, when electricity and indoor plumbing were luxuries that few rural people enjoyed, and when school lunches were most often paid for with quarts of home-canned tomatoes or beans, thousands of school children, with enthusiasm born of their first introduction to great music, contributed their nickles and dimes to sustain, of all things, a symphony orchestra.

The North Carolina Symphony was unique from its beginning. Originally subsidized as a musicians' employment program by the federal government during the New Deal, its first leader and organizer was a Pulitzer Prize winner, Lamar Stringfield. When government support was no longer forthcoming, when the idea of a state orchestra was all but abandoned, Ben and Maxine Swalin saw to it that the mission would continue. Determined that the joy of good music should be brought not just to black-tie audiences in acoustically attuned concert halls but to all the people, the orchestra trav-

Governor and Mrs. Terry Sanford at the Symphony Ball
(Reprinted from Raleigh Times, *May 23, 1964, by permission of The News*
and Observer Publishing Co., Raleigh, North Carolina; photo by Eddie Booker)

eled by bus and played in factories, schoolhouses, and churches across the hundreds of miles from the Outer Banks to the deep reaches of the Blue Ridge and the Great Smoky Mountains.

A vital network of loyal believers and supporters was established across the state. Even the thinning ranks of their musicians during World War II did not diminish their determination. On they went to scrounge the money, to attract the good musicians, to forge an enduring institution.

The recounting of the odyssey is as amusing as it is exciting. It is as readable for students no older than those first thrilled by the Symphony's children's concerts as it is for the older enthusiast of North Carolina history or the progress of the arts, or both.

The first paragraph of their Duke University honorary degree citation sums up the accomplishments of the two around whom this chronicle is set: "Benjamin Franklin Swalin and Martha Maxine Swalin, we honor you today as collaborators in the advancement of musical culture in the pioneering venture of building a symphony orchestra for the state of North Carolina. Your enthusiasm, noble aspirations, and untiring efforts not only developed the North Carolina Symphony into a nationally prominent musical organization, but brought to countless students in North Carolina an appreciation for great music."

When they retired after thirty-five years of leadership, Ben and Maxine Swalin left an orchestra of major importance and a musical experience and understanding that had enriched the vital spirit of North Carolina. Their recollections are an important part of our history.

Although it was not written for that purpose, this is truly a human story of two people. But for Ben Swalin, the North Carolina Symphony would not be. But for Maxine, Ben would not have prevailed.

Bravo!

Terry Sanford

Preface

I CAN still see that little girl's dancing eyes.

The sun was setting as our North Carolina Symphony bus turned off the highway onto the graveled entrance to stop before the small country motel. The child, excited at the sudden arrival of so many strangers, had ventured nearer to watch, eyes wide and questioning, as the musicians piled out carrying bags, unloading instruments—horns, drums, strings, the lot.

One of the musicians noticed her.

"Honey, do you live around here?"

She turned to face him, beaming. "Yes, sir"—she pointed toward a frame house a hundred yards away—"right over yonder 'side the hard-circus road."

"The hard-circus road?"

"Yes, sir. That big road over yonder you all just been ridin' on."

"Oh yes." His puzzled expression warmed to a grin. "I see. That hard-circus road right over there."

I hadn't said anything, but I'd been watching and listening. "If ever I get around to writing a book recording our experiences, Maxine's and mine and the North Carolina Symphony's," I said to myself as I picked up our bags to go inside, "I've already got the perfect title for it. Little girl, you don't know it, but you have just named that book."

"Hard-circus" road. The road we'd just been ridin' on. Hard-surface roads, miles upon hundreds of miles, asphalt and concrete, unyielding, frigidly cold, steaming hot, straight, curving, twisting, ascending steeply, falling away fast to the flatlands, unrolling for us changing panoramas of sights and sounds and places and people.

Never did I see that child again.

But now, little girl, here is that book for which you provided the title—an apt one, I think—and to you and all the other boys and girls who have grown up with the North Carolina Symphony I happily dedicate it.

O V E R the years and lengthening miles of that road of experience so charmingly designated by that little girl—indeed, since before my involvement with the North Carolina Symphony—I have continued to ponder the meaning of the musical art as an expression of the human will, and for me the search in itself has become essentially one of human perceptions and spiritual values.

So I have resolved to record here what I, an American, have felt as a student and teacher grappling with the problem of building within our culture something new and different. This experience has generated in me, and in my associates in the musical and scholarly adventure of the Symphony, a wealth of exciting and stimulating ideas.

The years of my preparation and training had embraced arduous work and risk, and in coming to North Carolina I would be venturing into a section of the nation to which I was not accustomed and at a time when our country was trying to rescue itself from the Great Depression only to be catapulted into World War II. The times were heavy and dark with restrictions and difficulties and everywhere there was the reminder that "resistance tests the soul." And yet, in those challenging years there would develop in North Carolina an idea new in musical tradition and history, certainly new and revolutionary in this state, when legislation enacted by the North Carolina General Assembly provided a recurring subsidy in support of a symphony orchestra—significant legislation that gave the Symphony not only financial support but also official recognition and respectability.

In drawing the blueprint for the North Carolina Symphony, it was realized early that there had to be discipline along with creative thinking—as expressed in the final line of Tennyson's *Ulysses*, we had "to strive, to seek, to find, and not to yield." In building this projected Orchestra for the People, there would be formidable obstacles to overcome. But there was hope, and there would be growing optimism, eagerness, and enthusiasm to confront the task.

The accomplishment of our task would require discovering and recruiting musical talent, organizing local membership chapters in the small towns and cities of the state, and developing a Children's Concert Division. Our successful efforts would lead to nationwide recognition, and to statewide fund-raising efforts that happily would culminate in the awarding by the Ford Foundation of a $1,000,000 grant contingent upon its being matched within the prescribed period of July 1, 1966–June 30, 1971.

That challenge was formidable. But despite the wide unrest and stringency of the times, the goal was reached. From a blueprint blurred and indistinct in places, the structure of a dream was building, rising upward and expanding outward and achieving form and stability. Music was spreading and reverberating from schoolhouses and churches tucked away in coves of the Blue Ridge and the Great Smokies to hamlets and fishing villages rimming the Atlantic, and over the broad expanse of the more populated Piedmont.

Acknowledgments

F o r the opportunity and assistance so generously given toward the completion of this book, I wish to acknowledge my indebtedness to Terry Sanford, to LeGette Blythe, to Sydenham B. Alexander, Jr., to Julia McVaugh, editor, and to my wife, Maxine.

Introduction
How I Came to North Carolina

M Y wife and I came to Chapel Hill in 1935 with no inkling that it was to be our permanent home.

I had been employed to teach in the second summer session that year at the University of North Carolina at the invitation of Dr. Glen Haydon. Glen Haydon and I had been students together in Vienna, both receiving our doctorates in 1932; he had then returned to the University of California at Berkeley to resume his teaching. We had enjoyed a reunion at a conference of the National Music Teachers' Assocation in the Midwest during the Christmas holidays of 1934.

Not long after that meeting, Dr. Haydon informed me that he had been selected to head the music department at the University of North Carolina. The previous administration had fallen upon difficult times, he said, and he was intent on rebuilding the department by inviting to his faculty scholars with Ph.D. degrees.

I was first on his list, he said. Would I accept a position teaching at the second summer session?

I accepted the summer school offer and reported to Glen Haydon in Chapel Hill. After I had been there a day or two, he asked me to play for a group of music enthusiasts that he had assembled. I believe I played the Bach *Chaconne* for solo violin, and perhaps one or two other selections. Dr. Haydon then evidently got in touch with Dr. Frank Porter Graham, president of the university, and I was invited to become a member of the faculty.

Acceptance of the invitation was not automatic, however, because at that time I was employed at DePauw University and I had appreciated my work there, even though my teaching load was approximately thirty-three hours per week. But the DePauw contracts had been delayed due to the severity of the Depression, and members of the faculty had no absolute assurance of employment for the coming fall session (although a promise had been made by the administration that contracts would be available in September). My salary at DePauw had been $3,000, whereas at Chapel Hill I would start at only $2,750. But at Chapel Hill there would be work with the University Orchestra, and courses and research in musicology—and I would be able to complete the rewriting of my book, *The Violin Concerto: A Study in German Romanticism* (published in 1941 by the University of North Carolina Press with the aid of a subsidy from the American Council of Learned Societies).

My decision could not be made until I had communicated with the president of DePauw University to inquire if I might be released from my forthcoming teaching obligations there. When the reply granting permission arrived, I accepted appointment as a member of the teaching staff of the University of North Carolina.

I BROUGHT to Chapel Hill a wide-ranging experience. After graduating in 1919 from North High School in Minneapolis, Minnesota, I had auditioned with Emil Oberhoffer, conductor of the Minneapolis Symphony Orchestra (now the Minnesota Symphony Orchestra), and became that orchestra's youngest member. During my two years with the orchestra, I learned a great deal from its experienced musicians; while on tour in Winnipeg, Canada, I bought a handsome Panormo violin, still one of my treasured possessions; and I developed a desire for a university education, inspired by the numerous stops made by our touring orchestra at colleges and universities.

However, my first need was for more violin training, and thus in the spring of 1921 I went to New York to study with the master pedagogue Franz Kneisel. I was privileged to study with him in private lessons for two years, and then at the Institute of Musical Art (which became the Juilliard School of Music). In New

York—and in Blue Hill, Maine, during the summers of 1921–23—I learned not only from my lessons with the great master but also from hearing some of the eminent violinists who were his friends and colleagues, and from the summer chamber music sessions that were an important part of the Kneisel discipline. After Franz Kneisel's untimely death in 1926, I studied with Professor Leopold Auer, who replaced Kneisel at the Institute of Musical Art.

In the meantime, I needed an income to help support my lessons. In the fall of 1921 I joined the first violin section of the Capitol Theater Orchestra, thanks to the recommendation of William Kroll, the concert-master. That job was just one of many, some short and some long. My New York "career" included some 300 performances of the show "Up She Goes," a remunerative job in the WOR Radio Orchestra, and giving private violin lessons to the daughter of novelist (and pianist) Professor John Erskine.

To feed my mind, I studied for the B.S., and then the M.A. in English literature, at Columbia University. In 1930 it was one of my professors at Columbia, Carl Van Doren, who encouraged me to leave my career in New York, which was educating me in many ways, and to accept an International Fellowship to Vienna for which I had applied that spring.

Knowing no one in Europe, and able to speak only a few sentences of German, I arrived in September 1930 at the Vienna Musikhochschule to study violin, composition, and conducting, along with courses at the University of Vienna ultimately leading to the Ph.D. degree. After two years of study under notable professors and exposure to excellent musical performances, I received the Ph.D. I then set out in January 1933 to visit various sections of Europe in which I had a special interest. In my travels—to Pisek, Czechoslovakia; to Berlin; to Sweden, the land of my parents; to Copenhagen; and to Cambridge—I sought out the scholars and musicians whose work I had admired, and I was fortunate to meet them.

Enriched, I returned to New York and the Depression—fearing that work would be hard to find for someone with no secretarial skills. However, before long I was engaged as Professor of Violin and Theory at DePauw University in Greencastle, Indiana. It was in the summer of my second year at DePauw that I made the move to North Carolina.

MORE important even than the experience that I brought to Chapel Hill was my companion-for-life, my bride Maxine. I had met Martha Maxine McMahon when we were both studying at the Institute of Musical Art, and I married her on January 1, 1935, after several years of being kept apart by too little money and too many miles. At the time of our wedding she was teaching in Iowa, and I, of course, was in Indiana—but in the summer of 1935 we packed our belongings in a single trunk and boarded the train together for North Carolina.

We were hardly settled in Chapel Hill before our courses diverged again. Maxine had been hoping to extend her graduate studies in music, and I agreed that it was important for her future. I was proud of her ambition. But even now, after five decades, I recall the loneliness I felt when she departed for a year at Radcliffe College and left me to "board out" in Chapel Hill.

In the years since her triumphant return with her master's degree, Maxine has been an essential part of my life and being. Without her, neither I nor the North Carolina Symphony could have accomplished what we did. As wife, she has been counselor, encourager, and supporter in many respects. As coworker, she has been the Symphony's pianist, harpsichordist, executive assistant, hostess, "advance man," children's concert coordinator and narrator, and whatever else was needed.

At evening concerts Maxine observed audience reactions, and her recommendations were an important part of the planning process for each new touring season. As planning progressed, the problems of logistics and repertoire would begin to sort themselves out, and soon another season with a variety of programs would be ready for the varied communities of North Carolina. After traveling thousands of miles to those communities, Maxine and I would be ready and grateful to return to Chapel Hill, to rest in the peace of our home in the woods, to watch our neighbor turn the red earth as he prepared his garden amid the blossoming wild plum and pear trees, and to salute, each morning, " . . . the wind that comes / And goes among the leaves and sings!"

F o r the many felicities of our life here we are indebted to the University of North Carolina, to the stimulating community of Chapel Hill, and to the wonderful people throughout this state. It is a source of great pride that in 1971 I was recognized by the University with the honorary degree of Doctor of Fine Arts. Eight years later, in 1979, when both Maxine and I were surprised and honored with individual Doctorates of Humane Letters by Duke University, we were both proud and humbled. But these honors belong equally to the people of North Carolina who shared and supported our dream. In the words of Paul Green's Christmas greeting:

> The dreams and deeds men set their hearts upon,
> We ask the witness of Thy love
> Upon this hour
> And on us all.

The Symphony's First Beginning

EARLY in this century, from Hatteras Light to Grandfather Mountain to the Tennessee border, the people of North Carolina seldom heard or saw a symphony orchestra. As a veteran alumnus of the state's oldest university once told me, "The violin in my day was a fiddlin' instrument, and a fellow would be ashamed to carry a violin case across the campus or even talk about a symphony orchestra."

But a young musician who returned to his native North Carolina in the 1920s brought with him a desire to share the wonder of music. Lamar Stringfield, born October 10, 1897, in the Wendell community a few miles east of Raleigh, had grown up in an era of developing economic depression and darkening gloom of war. He had attended college at Mars Hill and Wake Forest. He had then served his country for three years, first in the N.C. Infantry on the Mexican border and then with the 105th Engineers in France, before going to New York for advanced study in flute and composition. I knew him slightly at the Institute of Musical Art when he was studying flute under Georges Barrere and I was studying with Franz Kneisel. There he won a prize in composition and his artist's diploma in 1924. While in New York he gained not only facility in performing and conducting under the tutelage of able teachers, but also practical experience that would be helpful in his later organizing and conducting efforts. Prior to his work with the North Carolina Symphony, Stringfield was invited to conduct orchestras in several American cities. In 1928 he was awarded the Pulitzer Prize in music for his orchestral suite, *From the Southern Mountains.*

The southern mountains inspired more than Stringfield's pen. "I had a wild dream," he confided to a friend, "of a symphony orchestra for Asheville, North Carolina." And so in the summer of 1927 he organized and conducted a "demonstration concert" in Asheville whose success led to more concerts that summer and in the two summers that followed. Stringfield, convinced that the entire state needed and deserved a symphony orchestra, then went to Raleigh to ask Gov. O. Max Gardner for state subsidy. The governor knew that the General Assembly had no funds to spare in those Depression days, and he rejected the plan. But the idea did not perish.

In 1930 Stringfield decided that North Carolina was where he wanted to live and work, and he came to Chapel Hill with the notion of forming a university department that would fill the common ground between the Department of Music, the Carolina Playmakers, and the Institute for Research in Social Science. That notion took form in 1931 as the Institute of Folk Music, whose threefold purpose was, as Stringfield later described it, to: "(1) collect and preserve native folk-lore through encouraging and guiding folk festivities; (2) encourage musical composition, stressing the value of folk-music as a basis; (3) discover and utilize in concert exceptional musical instrumentalists and develop in them sound musicianship."

The concerts that were organized by Stringfield at the Institute of Folk Music brought together musicians who developed an enthusiasm for the idea of a statewide symphony orchestra, and conviction grew that the state had sufficient musicians with the talent and experience to form such an orchestra. Further support for the idea came from the North Carolina Ten-Year Plan, Incorporated, established in 1931 to improve the economic and cultural resources of the state. Tyre C. Taylor, director of the Plan, felt that a statewide orchestra would help to attract tourists to North Carolina.

On February 19, 1932, at Tyre Taylor's suggestion, a meeting was called in the office of Dr. Frank Porter Graham, president of the university. The meeting unanimously adopted Mr. Taylor's motion to form the North Carolina Symphony Society in order to further the establishment of a North Carolina Symphony Orchestra. Those present at the meeting agreed to act as a steering committee to organize the Society, and they did their work well: by December 31, 1932, when the North Carolina Symphony Society was incorporated as a nonprofit organization, it was able to list 667 charter members. (Steering committee members are listed in Appendix A.)

On March 21 a second meeting was held, at which Col. Joseph Hyde Pratt, a graduate of Yale who had been professor of geology at Chapel Hill from 1904 to 1925 (and state geologist most of that time), an officer in World War I, and a distinguished humanitarian, was named president of the new society, and Lamar Stringfield, flutist, conductor, and composer, was handed the challenging task of organizing and conducting the projected symphony orchestra. It was decided that the orchestra should plan an early demonstration concert, and on May 14, 1932, after five rehearsals, forty-eight musicians comprising the North Carolina Symphony Orchestra presented in Chapel Hill a program of compositions by Wagner, Beethoven, Stoessel, Borodin, and Tchaikovsky.

News of the birth of an orchestra spread quickly, as evidenced by a letter to Colonel Pratt, dated May 5, 1932, from a representative of the Salter management in Budapest:

Dear Sir,

Your plans regarding the formation of a new orchestra gives me occasion to write to you, as I have been 15 years long the European General representative of the New York Metropolitan Opera Company and as I know the artistic conditions in America very well.

I am since long time in conection with all first class German conductors and I suppose that you have also the intention, like it is in all great American cities to take a German condutor. But in case you would prefer to have an Italian man I could bring you the Italian artist who is comparised by the Italians to be better than Toscanini hem selfe.

*Colonel Joseph Hyde Pratt, first president of the
North Carolina Symphony Society
(Courtesy of the North Carolina Collection, UNC Library at Chapel Hill)*

If somebody of you would come over to Europe, I could travel with hem from one city to the other one.

Therefore it would be very good, if you would be kind enough to cable me your intention.

I also could make you an offer with names.

With best regards your truly. . . .

But contrary to the agent's insistence that North Carolina, "like it is in all great American cities," should have a German conductor, or perhaps "an Italian man," North Carolina's Lamar Stringfield directed the first demonstration concert and the eight that followed in five different cities during the Symphony's first two seasons. The orchestra supported itself for two years with concert receipts, individual contributions, and society memberships. *The musicians were not paid,* however; their only remuneration, as one of them expressed it, was "the joy of playing together," along with their actual expenses.

In 1934, under the auspices of the Institute of Folk Music, the North Carolina Symphony applied to the Federal Emergency Relief Administration (FERA), and in May of that year it was awarded a grant of $45,000. Concert programs carried an announcement explaining the project (see Appendix B).

The orchestra's performances were received with great enthusiasm, and the project was praised in high and hopeful terms in the newspapers of the state. By September 1935, it was estimated that its members, playing in groups ranging in size from trio to full orchestra, had given more than 140 concerts in some fifty towns and cities in North Carolina—and every concert had included at least one work by an American composer. Stringfield's interest in popularizing folk music as a source of entertainment and of compositional inspiration was evident in the programs, and was one of the reasons for their wide appeal.

The printed programs for the 1935 summer season included an optimistic statement that the musicians in the orchestra would become self-supporting, and that North Carolina would retain the orchestra as a social, cultural, and economic asset to its people.

Visiting conductors, such as Hans Kindler and Percy Grainger, spoke warmly of the Symphony's musicianship and aims. A noted composer and pianist, John Powell of Richmond, who had been active in organizing the Symphony Society and who joined the orchestra as guest artist in a performance of one of his compositions in August 1935, was later reported in the *Charlotte Observer* as saying: "If the people of North Carolina allow this orchestra to die, it will be because of ignorance, inertia, or indifference. There is not another organization like it in the world."

Unfortunately, however, in the fall and winter of 1935 a crisis situation developed, which soon brought the cosponsorship roles of the North Carolina Symphony Society and the FERA to a close. Lamar Stringfield was appointed regional director of the Works Progress Administration (WPA) Federal Music Project; but strangely, although his region included North Carolina and his office was in Raleigh, he was officially ordered to have nothing to do with the North Carolina program. The governmental administration of the Symphony became fragmented and confused. The orchestra split into two units, one in Asheville and one in Durham, which became "fighting units" at war with each other over their musical directorship and with the WPA over their administration. The FERA was slow in setting up proper papers of transfer to the WPA for the musicians, with the result that they went without pay for several weeks. Stormy sessions took place among the musicians, and among Symphony Society officials and Regional Director Stringfield.

The inevitable break was signaled in messages such as the letter of December 4, 1935, to Lamar Stringfield from Gerald Bryant, concert-master of the North Carolina Symphony and assistant director of projects, who wrote, in part:

Monday afternoon Mr. Schwartz came to the rehearsal and notified the orchestra of the fact that their checks would not be available before Saturday or possibly Monday. . . . The members of the orchestra told me unless something was done they would pawn their instruments which meant no rehearsals for the coming week or week and a half.

A week later, on December 11, 1935, Stringfield wrote to Col. Joseph Hyde Pratt, the Symphony Society's president:

> . . . More important, even after this pay is straightened out . . . is the reviving of spirit among the personnel and re-establishing a leadership which will be congenial. . . . So far, the directors of the present project absolutely ignore the fact that the Society exists . . . and that I still am the Musical Director as appointed by the executive committee. . . .

Experimental appointments by the FERA to provide overseers and substitute conductors only brought further dissension among the players. There appeared to be no likelihood of resolving the impasse. On January 3, 1936, three weeks after Stringfield's pessimistic letter to him, Colonel Pratt wrote from the Brighton Hotel in Washington to Bruce McClure, the WPA's Director of Professional Projects:

> Considering the lack of unity of those in charge of the N.C. Symphony Orchestra Project, and the fact that nothing definite has been accomplished with this project during the past three months, it has been considered wise to withdraw the sponsorship of the N.C. Symphony Society for this project.
> The Society is interested in this project and will gladly again sponsor such a project, if another is inaugurated from Washington.

Although the Society was compelled to withdraw its sponsorship of the project because of the dissension and the failure of accomplishment during the last months of 1935, and although in North Carolina as elsewhere throughout the nation there were rumblings of dissatisfaction with the administration of various public assistance projects, I would like to point out that the FERA, in establishing direct grants from the federal government, had by 1934 been able to provide sorely needed public assistance to more than twenty million people in the United States. And under the WPA Harry Hopkins set up Federal Arts Projects embracing the Federal Theater and Federal Music Project for actors, painters, and musicians. The WPA employed 15,000 jobless musicians, including composers, and established three symphony orchestras—Utah, Buffalo, and Oklahoma—that are active even today. It created theatrical organizations such as the Barter Theater of Virginia, and art works by Jackson Pollock, Stuart Davis, Arshile Gorky, and others.

Nevertheless, in the years 1936–38 the North Carolina Symphony, now a Federal Music Project of the WPA, was having to struggle to keep going. In Asheville, Joseph DeNardo worked mightily to keep at least that unit of the orchestra together. In May 1938 I was guest conductor at a Greensboro performance in which Harold Cone of Greensboro was soloist (in the Schumann *Piano Concerto in A Minor*). That summer the orchestra gave a series of concerts in the Harbor Island Auditorium at Wrightsville Beach, conducted by Dr. Laird Waller of Chicago. But shortly thereafter the Symphony was disbanded as a federal project, some of its members being sent to Richmond to join the Virginia unit under Dr. Waller, and others scattering to various jobs within North Carolina.

In the fall of 1938 I was invited to address a teachers' meeting in Raleigh, and I was asked about the Symphony. I asserted that "the old North Carolina Symphony has fallen into desuetude."

Immediately a hand shot up, and I was interrupted by Erle Stapleton, a director of the Federal Music Project.

"The North Carolina Symphony did not fall into desuetude," he declared. "It was a government relief project of the Works Progress Administration, and only those musicians who could qualify for relief were eligible for admission to the orchestra. But since the purpose of the project had been fulfilled, the orchestra was discontinued."

The Second Beginning

SHORTLY after my arrival in Chapel Hill in 1935 I was standing near the post office building downtown when a large white Cadillac went by. My companion informed me that it belonged to Lamar Stringfield, "you know, the conductor of the North Carolina Symphony." That was the first I had heard of the Symphony, or of Stringfield's presence in North Carolina. At that time, the dream of a viable state symphony was already starting to fade.

My responsibilities in the music department included directing the University Orchestra, and I gradually developed the notion of strengthening that group by merging it with the remains of the WPA orchestra. I knew that such a project would require an adequate rehearsal hall and a source of funds, and I was not sure how these could be acquired. Nor was I sure how I could fit it into my teaching schedule. But it seemed a notion worth pursuing, and by early 1937 I had formulated a proposal to reestablish a permanent North Carolina Symphony Orchestra under the auspices of the North Carolina Symphony Society. That spring I went to Washington, D.C., to discuss the plan with Colonel Pratt of the Symphony Society, and he was entirely supportive. I then consulted with Erle Stapleton, state director of the Federal Music Project, who also approved the idea and promised WPA cooperation in moving the project to Chapel Hill if the university agreed to the merger.

It looked as though we might be on our way! On April 24, 1937, I wrote to Colonel Pratt with the glad news that the Women's

Federation of Music Clubs of North Carolina had passed a resolution supporting the North Carolina State Symphony Orchestra; that Director Stapleton was on our side; and that a sample concert was scheduled for May 24 in Chapel Hill. This concert, I hoped, would convince the university community of the worth of my idea.

My proposal had pointed out that from the approximately thirty players in the WPA orchestra, ten or fifteen might become students in the University's music department and members of the University Symphony.

But it was not to be.

Five weeks later—May 30, 1937—in a letter to Colonel Pratt I reported the flat rejection of my plan by the head of the music department, Dr. Haydon. His terse statement rejecting it had been read to a small group of original supporters and officers of the North Carolina Symphony Society, including Fred B. McCall, Hugo Giduz, Robert Linker, and Felix Grisette. It indicated clearly that our "efforts and aims" were "not desirable so far as they relate to Chapel Hill and the University." There had been no discussion beforehand, and there was little need for it afterward. I would find out later that Dean Robert House and President Graham, who had requested that an *open* meeting be called to discuss the matter, had never seen my plan for the merger. I further reported to Colonel Pratt: "You can imagine that my position here is strained and difficult."

I was disappointed and puzzled. As I had said in an earlier letter to Colonel Pratt, I could not understand the reasoning of Dr. Haydon that the presence of professional musicians would be a "distraction" to university music students. If our students aren't to be given training qualifying them to be performing musicians, I wondered, how are they to advance to professional standards? And how would entrance of the Federal Music Project *impede* the normal growth of student activity?

This defeat was a definite setback, but I was still determined to explore every possible way of reviving and rebuilding the old North Carolina Symphony Orchestra. That same year I accepted an invitation to a meeting in Winston-Salem convoked in an effort to save "the remnants of the WPA Orchestra project." Although the ultimate purpose was to obtain matching funds in order to secure additional support of the relief project and the meeting that day was primarily a business session, a group of WPA musicians—perhaps twenty or twenty-five—presented a brief musical program.

"The people do not care for that kind of music," an official of one of the large corporations in Winston-Salem asserted after the musicians had performed. "They want hillbilly."

His pretentious statement irritated me, and I was quick to challenge it.

"Do you have a son enrolled in the University at Chapel Hill?" I asked him.

"Yes, I do."

"Then are you suggesting that the University eliminate courses in mathematics, physics, chemistry, philosophy, Shakespeare, and other serious and difficult subjects?"

"Of course not," he replied. "Those courses are necessary."

"But what if the students do not care for such studies? What if we provided only those courses they think they should take?" I persisted. "Put a burlesque show on Franklin Street and then offer them only the courses and the music they *think they want*"—my tone, I confess, was sarcastic—"and there will be little need for more than hillbilly entertainment."

I then proceeded to define education as the "subordination of our so-called likes and dislikes in the attainment of high, rational, and aesthetic objectives calculated to uplift our people." But I—and my high, rational, and aesthetic definition—did not prevail that day.

(There was a considerable Chapel Hill contingent at that meeting, including several members of the music department and some of their wives. Maxine was seated next to one of the wives, who happened to be a scientist. When an impassioned gentleman declared from the podium, "We *have* to save this orchestree," Maxine's neighbor leaned over and whispered: "What kind of tree is an orchestree?" Maxine retorted: "You tell me. *You're* the botanist!")

WITH the demise of the WPA project in the fall of 1938, and with the negative attitude on the part of the University's music department, it seemed that the North Carolina Symphony Society had failed in its self-appointed mission. Its members were not prepared to admit defeat, however, and neither was I.

The Greensboro program of May 1938, in which I was guest conductor, had brought me a communication from Edward B. Benjamin of Greensboro and New Orleans, who had attended the concert and heard the performance with satisfaction. Even though he realized that some of our players were relatively inexperienced, he believed they had performed better than some musicians in professional symphony orchestras. And he wondered if we could "build an orchestra that would become self-sustaining financially." I replied that I did not believe a symphony *could sustain* itself, but I hoped nevertheless that we could build a good orchestra.

That year Mr. Benjamin invited Maxine and me to have Thanksgiving dinner with him and his lovely wife in their Greensboro home. That visit—and the memorably delicious dinner—marked the day the Benjamins became our cherished friends. And afterward I would reflect upon my hopes, as expressed to him, of our building a good symphony orchestra, even though it could not sustain itself financially. Why shouldn't such an achievement be possible, I reasoned. Why might we not be able to reactivate some talent in North Carolina and infuse new ideas for a *new* orchestra?

The dream simply wouldn't die. Colonel Pratt, Edward Benjamin, and our loyal friends in Chapel Hill all hoped that it could become a reality, and I was convinced that a new start could and should be made. Finally, on December 21, 1939, a dinner meeting was held in Chapel Hill to revive and reorganize the Symphony Society; Colonel Pratt was again elected president, Robert Linker was elected treasurer, and I was appointed musical director of the Society and conductor of the orchestra.

With the assistance of Maxine and of Albin Pikutis, one of my violin students who had followed me from DePauw, I gathered together several musicians from the University Orchestra (which was then woefully weak) and other musicians wherever we could locate them, along with a few former WPA players. A basic principle of faith of the new organization was our resolve to pay for all musical services no matter how modest the compensation, and happily there were few complaints in those days. Unhappily, there was virtually no money. But we did have friends.

One of those friends was Paul Green, one of the original Carolina Playmakers, who had been one of the first Chapel Hillians to welcome Maxine and me to the University community. I had been with him on only a few occasions before I began distinctly to sense that, in the parlance of the 1930s, we were on the same wavelength—and Paul, I'm confident, shared that feeling.

Paul was already on his way to establishing his place as a dramatist: he had won the Pulitzer Prize for drama (in 1927), and had produced the first in a notable series of symphonic dramas, *The Lost Colony* (in 1937—with music by Lamar Stringfield). He was also a liberal, ready and determined in every opportunity to defend and champion the hungry, the hurt, the ignored, the ill-treated. And early I discovered him to be—happily for me and importantly for his fellow Tar Heels—not only an artist of great talent but also one enthusiastically and effectively supportive of artists and the arts.

Another good friend to me and to the Symphony was Mrs. Athol C. Burnham, "Johnsie" to her friends, who had been one of the first woman violinists to play with the Metropolitan Opera Orchestra in New York. She had returned to her native North Carolina after the death of her husband and settled in Chapel Hill, and she had played occasionally in the early Symphony before it became a relief project. She continued her active work in music, studying violin with me— and enthusiastically supporting the North Carolina Symphony.

The new orchestra would require some tympani and other equipment, and we calculated that our initial operating expenses would amount to $200. So Paul, Johnsie, and I went to the Bank of Chapel Hill together and borrowed the money. One hurdle had been cleared.

But many hurdles remained. We still had no rehearsal home, office, secretarial help, publicity chairman, personnel director, or business manager. We even had some difficulty in using the name

Johnsie Burnham and Paul Green recalling the early days of the Symphony
(Photo by Maury Faggart)

"North Carolina Symphony" because there were various indications of financial indebtedness and broken promises, which brought with them some prejudice. Since we had received no minutes from the years 1932–39, we had only a vague idea of the orchestra's early business operations. The few sketchy, incomplete records that we inherited indicated that some membership dues had never been accounted for. Those people in North Carolina who had been supportive of the old orchestra now considered it defunct and beyond hope of resurrecting, and the music library of the WPA orchestra had already been given to the University of North Carolina music department.

Like most public cultural organizations, our emerging Symphony drew its early support from a few friends with modest financial resources. Although more and more people were contributing their time and efforts, there was still the financial burden of creating and developing an orchestra with its complexities and problems. Paul Green knew from experience the heartbreaking task of making a dream come true while his epic *The Lost Colony* was taking form on Roanoke Island.

The times were heavy with adjustments and undercurrents of worldwide unrest. I had passed my first physical examination for military service and was planning to join the armed services. However, I turned thirty-eight a few days before the issuance of an Army order that men of thirty-eight would not be eligible for enlistment at that time. And for the orchestra there were limitations in travel and in rehearsal time, along with a shifting personnel. Nevertheless, on March 16, 1940, the new North Carolina Symphony Orchestra gave its first formal concert. I shall never forget that date or the place, the Meredith College auditorium in Raleigh. The program included the *Euryanthe Overture* by Weber and Haydn's *Symphony No. 104 in D Major* ("London"); the press criticism was favorable, and the concert netted receipts of approximately $90!

The few recorded figures available to me as we undertook rebuilding the orchestra revealed the stringency of the times. The Society's bank balance from May 1, 1935, to January 1, 1940, was $3.64. There were no other assets, and the few remnants that we inherited from various sources from 1932 to 1939 were later turned over to the State Archives along with the programs of the orchestra's early concerts. After Albin Pikutis became treasurer, he deposited $296 in February 1940, which brought our total cash assets apparently to $424.64.

Following our March concert we printed a promotional leaflet stating our aims, quoting our press notices, and soliciting memberships:

A Symphony Orchestra, like a university, high school, and library, is not self-supporting. Realizing this, the North Carolina Symphony Society has begun a membership campaign with a goal of $25,000 to insure the establishment of the orchestra upon a substantial basis. The Society hopes to secure at least 100 members in each county of the state, and asks for your endorsement and support through its several classes of membership. . . .

The classes of membership ranged from $1 ("Active") to $1,000 ("Benefactor")

W E felt that we were on our way. The orchestra was able to obtain engagements that year to play in Chapel Hill, Fayetteville, Statesville, and Asheville. The Asheville concert, fortunately for us, was broadcast by radio. Earlier we had received a jolting letter from an Asheville citizen who evidently took considerable pride in his understanding and appreciation of orchestral music. He had written us that he would do all he could to *prevent* the organization of a North Carolina Symphony *unless* it could begin with a budget of $100,000 and become as formidable as the New York Philharmonic. He declared that there was already "too much musical mediocrity in North Carolina," and he was going to do nothing to add to it.

But this gentleman decided to attend our concert when he learned that we would perform in Asheville. On his way that afternoon he turned on his car radio and was listening to orchestral music as he drove into the parking lot at the Civic Auditorium. He turned off the car engine but, intrigued, continued to sit in the car and listen to the music until a friend who had just come from the auditorium noticed him.

"Hey, you're missing some good music," his friend said. "The concert has already started. How come you aren't going inside?"

"I meant to," the other man answered, "but I'm getting better music on the radio. It must be the New York Philharmonic."

The friend leaned in to listen.

"New York Philharmonic the dickens! That's the North Carolina Symphony, and you'd hear 'em better if you went inside!"

Later, that Asheville man became one of the orchestra's staunch supporters.

During the ensuing months, we sensed the increase of genuine good will among the orchestra personnel along with a growing determination to play good music. Preeminent in our thinking was the opportunity we were enjoying of contact with great music and with musicians who wanted to study and play together. Although some of the musicians had enlisted in the nation's armed forces, there were capable players from college faculties, and others who were sometimes available at the conclusion of their limited seasons in professional orchestras such as the St. Louis, Kansas City, Atlanta, and Minneapolis symphonies.

Our concerts were rewarding too. Highlights of 1941 include a concert in Greensboro, with the Kerenoff Ballet, in support of "Bundles for Britain"; the first children's concert by the new orchestra; and a May concert in Chapel Hill where we presented the same program as that given at our debut concert at Meredith College in Raleigh the year before, adding Wagner's *Siegfried's Rhine Journey* and Mozart's *Symphonie Concertante* (K.364), with soloists Benjamin Swalin, violinist, and Julia Mueller, violist. (Mrs. Mueller was distinguished not only for her musicianship, but also for her capacity as an administrator both at the North Carolina School of the Arts and in Duke University's music department. Her sudden death in 1979 was a severe loss to North Carolina musicians and to a wide public.)

We were developing a rehearsal routine that in large measure was responsible for whatever success the orchestra was able to achieve. The members of the orchestra lived in Chapel Hill, Charlotte, Raleigh, Asheville, Durham, Kinston, Greenville, Wilmington—all over North Carolina. This made it very difficult to get together for rehearsals, and even for scheduled concerts. Our concerts almost invariably were scheduled for weekends. Prior to each concert we made detailed arrangements for lodging and rehearsal space, and we would see that each of the musicians received the necessary information. On the weekend of the concert we would all arrive at the designated place, perhaps a school auditorium or gymnasium, for rehearsal on Friday afternoon or evening and again on Saturday. This might be our only opportunity to go over the entire program together, and by itself it would not have been enough to ensure a polished performance. What made the crucial difference was that smaller groups of musicians would get together on the weekends between concerts whenever and wherever we could. In Charlotte I could meet with five or six musicians in the Parker-Gardner store, next door to the old S & W Cafeteria. The next week I might go to Asheville and rehearse a small group. And the following week perhaps to the Greensboro–High Point area or the eastern part of the state.

Vividly I remember those early months—and years—of the newly resurrected North Carolina Symphony. They were tough times, when our hard-circus road seemed interminably steep and we had to struggle to continue ascending it. And always there was the nagging, frustrating dearth of funds. The musicians paid their own travel expenses and the cost was often burdensome—from Charlotte to Chapel Hill and return, for example, or from Asheville to Raleigh or Kinston and return. We were giving several concerts each year, and to each of the concerts the musicians were contributing two, three, or sometimes four or five days of their time (even though most of them were regularly employed in various capacities). It was time freely contributed.

There was no such thing as a regular salary for our services. But sometimes, as one of the orchestra's alumni recalls,

> We'd get what they called an "honorarium." It wasn't much, maybe ten dollars. The word sounded bigger anyway than the money was. One night after the concert—in Chapel Hill, I think it was—I heard a couple of the musicians discussing the hard times.
>
> "Have you got your honorarium yet?" one inquired of the other.
>
> "I'm not interested in anything like that," he answered. "What I want to know is when are we going to get our money?"

That indeed was the question we all wanted answered. When would the North Carolina Symphony Orchestra be assured of receiving financial support sufficient to permit its developing and maintaining a program of consistently high quality?

CHAPTER 3

A Milestone
The Horn-Tootin' Bill

W H E N our "new" orchestra was a fledgling and was having a difficult time gaining recognition as a viable musical organization, we
gained a valuable friend in Mrs. Charles E. Johnson of Raleigh, an
effective leader in the civic and cultural groups and activities in the
state. Mrs. Johnson heard the Symphony in concert in Raleigh's
Memorial Auditorium in 1942 (as part of the Raleigh Sesquicen-
tennial Celebration), and she then wrote a letter to the newspaper
in which she castigated the public for its indifference and praised
highly the work of the Symphony.

Publication of her letter delighted us, and it marked the beginning of our collaborating in the successful development of the orchestra project and program. Mrs. Johnson later became president
of the North Carolina Symphony Society, and she continued faithfully and enthusiastically to champion the orchestra.

In the fall of 1942 Mrs. Johnson accompanied Maxine and me to
the Governor's Mansion on what we considered an important and
special mission. She had arranged for an appointment with Governor and Mrs. J. Melville Broughton. We proposed to discuss with
the governor our growing conviction that the North Carolina Symphony Orchestra, if it were to be successful, would have to develop
into a basic educational institution with an exalted purpose similar
to a public school or a public library. And like public schools and
public libraries—this was the foundation stone we were proposing

to set—it should be sustained through inclusion in the North Carolina state budget with adequate biennial appropriations.

We discussed with Governor Broughton our hopes for the Symphony and our various ideas of how the hopes might be accomplished, emphasizing our contention that the General Assembly should provide funds for its support. He seemed to like our presentation, with the result that he and Mrs. Broughton joined Mrs. Johnson, Johnsie Burnham, and other friends of the Symphony in working for passage of legislation designed to help materially in accomplishing our goals.

For the supporters and partisans of the symphony, March 8, 1943, will long be remembered as a date of historical significance. That was the day that an American state by duly enacted legislation recognized a symphony orchestra, even as a quasi-state agency, by placing it under the "patronage and control of the state."

The piece of legislation enacted that day was Senate Bill No. 248. Early that morning Attorney General Harry McMullan had telephoned to ask me to come to Raleigh. Our bill, he said, was coming up for action by the General Assembly and it was important that I go over the proposed legislation carefully to see that it was worded precisely as I desired it. I told Mr. McMullan that although I appreciated his asking me, I felt it would be preferable for him to see to the final wording of the bill so that it would carry out his own ideas, "and," I added, "because you are familiar with budgetary requests."

Mrs. Giles Cover of Andrews, a member of the House of Representatives, presented the bill. During the debate prior to its passage, one legislator is reported to have said that as he was on his way to Raleigh from his home community, he passed a woman working in a field.

"I thought to myself, that poor soul could have a son in World War II," he shouted to his fellow legislators. "What would *she* say if she heard that I voted for this horn-tootin' bill?"

The appellation stayed with it, but Senate Bill No. 248 passed, and became a cultural milestone. Later Governor Broughton said at a luncheon in Chapel Hill that the passage of that bill was something of which he was proud, something for which he would be remembered.

The appropriation was only $2,000 for each year of the 1943–45 biennium. But passage of the legislation was a major victory for us and we rejoiced in our new importance, our *officially recognized* importance. After the bill became law there were some minor changes in our organization, but they were not substantive. Among other positive things, the bill prescribed that annual fiscal reports of the North Carolina Symphony should be available to the General Assembly through the state auditor's office.

Our "horn-tootin'" Senate Bill No. 248 soon became an inspiration for other organizations, because it purveyed what was evidently the first recurring appropriation to a symphony orchestra from a state government. So far as we could discover, there was no other state subvention for a symphony orchestra except for the Indianapolis Symphony, which was granted an appropriation for a specific number of children's performances per year. Later, when I made that assertion on NBC's "Monitor" program broadcast from New York, the governor of Vermont protested to North Carolina's Governor Luther Hodges. He insisted that the Vermont Symphony was the first orchestra to receive a state subvention, because in 1939 it had been granted a subsidy of $1,000 to enable it to play at the World's Fair in New York. That appropriation, of course, was quite different from the one given our symphony, which was a *recurring* subsidy. It was not until 1945, I believe, that the Vermont Symphony began receiving a regular appropriation from the Vermont state treasury.

W E later adopted the practice of playing a biennial "thank-you" concert for the legislators in the House Chambers. At these concerts, to demonstrate what the legislative appropriation was accomplishing for the children of the state, we would sometimes display music-inspired paintings by the children, or we might play a tape of children singing along at one of our school concerts, or occasionally we would invite an outstanding high school chorus to perform with

*The Little Symphony and the High Point A Capella Choir serenading the
North Carolina legislators
(Courtesy of the North Carolina Department of Archives and History)*

us. The year that we performed parts of Mendelssohn's *Elijah* with
students from High Point and Durham, we had to exert considerable ingenuity to fit everyone in. The combined choruses stood on
platforms between and around the pillars, and the instrumentalists
crowded together on the lowest level.

These concerts were always well received by the legislators, and
were sometimes reported in the press. In 1951, our evening concert
in the General Assembly was preceded by a matinee performance in
the auditorium of the Raleigh state prison. This resulted in a published news item that the orchestra had played for the *lawbreakers* in
the morning and for the *lawmakers* in the evening—presumably,
another North Carolina "first"!

The War—And Other Problems

IN September 1943 the Symphony Society's constitution and by-laws were still in a formative state, and I requested that a three-year contract be drawn up for me with my remuneration placed at one dollar per year. The board agreed, but with the provision that "when and as the Society's treasury had money," my remuneration would be increased until it reached a "level of respectability" in keeping with the dignity of the position.

The next two years for the orchestra were a period of intensive effort and expansion. By the end of the biennium—July 1, 1943 through June 30, 1945—for which the first appropriation had been made, the work of the orchestra had become better known and newspaper and magazine articles were drawing national attention to North Carolina's cultural leadership. In 1942 we had inaugurated a new educational program with a system of local committees (later called "chapters"). Each interested community was encouraged to form its own committee and sell sufficient memberships to ensure its own concert, with the promise of a free children's matinee as a bonus.

In our 1943 season the orchestra gave five performances with a budget of $13,257. During the 1944 season, six of fourteen programs were given for school children; but because of travel restrictions and the limited availability of players, eleven other invitations had to be declined. Japan's bombing of Pearl Harbor had been an assault also on our orchestra, which lost forty-five musicians through military conscription. It appeared that our Symphony might soon be decimated. If it was to survive, we realized, it would be necessary to locate and rehearse capable replacements.

We were fortunate to find a group of experienced musicians in the Richmond, Virginia, area. That meant I would have to go to Richmond to rehearse with them, and that presented problems. On one occasion I had to sleep in the railroad station there because there was no hotel space! Generally, though, because it was possible to rehearse with the Richmond contingent only on Sundays, I would leave Chapel Hill early on a Sunday morning, park my car at the Seaboard railway station in Raleigh, and board a 7:30 train for Richmond. The coaches usually were crowded with military personnel, mothers with fretful babies, and piles of bulky baggage. On arrival at Richmond I would barely have time for lunch at the John Marshall Hotel before going up to the roof of the hotel for a rehearsal at two o'clock. Following the rehearsal, someone would drive me to the station to catch a 5:00 train for Raleigh, where I was due to arrive at about 9:30 that night. Driving the thirty miles home to Chapel Hill, I'd have time to reflect upon the happenings of an exciting day in the Virginia capital. I liked the music and the new musical fellowship, and once I was almost tempted to accept an offer to take over the task of developing the Richmond symphony. But I declined because of the stronger urging of my teaching duties at the University in Chapel Hill that were continuing full-time.

Not until after I had taught my classes on Fridays was I able to travel to rehearse the different orchestra units over the state. There was precious little time for doing what had to be done, and none for leisure. But we had George Washington Carver's formula to inspire us: when someone asked the famed scientist how he had managed to develop from the lowly peanut and sweet potato such a wealth and range of useful products, he is reported to have said, "You have to take what you have and make something out of it."

Surely that was the story of our orchestra.

One Friday afternoon I drove the seventeen miles from Chapel Hill to Hillsborough, where I planned to park my car at a service station and catch the bus for Asheville for a weekend of rehearsals.

Just as I was arriving in Hillsborough, I saw the Asheville bus slowing to stop. Realizing that I had no time to find a parking spot and lock my car, I stopped in front of the gas pump, jumped out, and hurled my car keys to an approaching attendant.

"I've got to catch that bus!" I yelled to the man. "Please take care of my car. I'll be back Sunday night!" And I jumped on the bus just as it was pulling out.

We had our rehearsal in Asheville with two hornists, one violinist, a 'cellist, one clarinetist, and one or two other players; and late Sunday I caught the bus for the trip home. And when we got to the service station at Hillsborough, my car was there.

T H E Symphony board, recognizing how hard we were working to stretch our resources, voted to increase its budgetary request for the second biennium to $10,150 per year. We explained our financial needs to the governor, Senator H. P. Taylor, Senator Thomas Pearsall, and other leaders of the General Assembly. However, the approved appropriation was but $4,000 a year, for the biennium commencing July 1, 1945.

The efforts of our supporters to strengthen the legislature's aid to the orchestra spurred the determination of its opponents, it appeared, and in November 1944 we were suddenly faced with a "roadblock" threatening to impede the orchestra's further progress or to force it entirely off the road. This roadblock was a letter of protest to President Frank P. Graham signed by H. Hugh Altvater, dean of the Music School of the Woman's College of the University of North Carolina at Greensboro, who had been authorized to prepare and transmit a three-page statement "summarizing the views" of a committee ostensibly consisting of the dean himself; James Christian Pfohl, of Davidson College; Dr. Katherine Gilbert, head of the Fine Arts Division at Duke University; and Dr. Glen Haydon, of the University of North Carolina at Chapel Hill.

The committee's statement declared that,

with the passing of need for federal subsidies to [professional] musicians, the WPA Orchestra died gradually. Following a short interim, a state orchestra of another type was assembled under the leadership of Dr. Benjamin F. Swalin of Chapel Hill. Members of this later orchestra are drawn from the faculties and student bodies of colleges and high schools in the state and, in smaller measure, from among other state musicians. . . .

. . . It is quite obvious that $2,000.00 annually [the state subsidy] would be inadequate for the support of a professional orchestra . . . [and] that a subsidy near to $100,000.00 would be required. . . .

. . . This statement has been prepared under belief that the time has arrived for reevaluation of state orchestra activities in relation to college work. . . .

. . . School musicians who are building North Carolina music do not have leisure time or surplus energy for attempts to build at the top as well as from the bottom. . . .

The committee claimed that "immediately before concerts, highly intensive full rehearsals are held in a chosen community, the hours of rehearsal sometimes running as high as fourteen within a two-day period," and that "the conductor's ambition [is] to present twenty programs annually."

The statement further spoke of students having been "persuaded to leave the home campus for an exhausting weekend of rehearsals," and stated that "the state orchestra regularly drains off the best talents in the local groups." Even faculty members were not spared, according to the committee; they returned from "long rehearsals of the state group in a state of exhaustion which withdraws quality from their teaching for as long as a week." And thus the state group "undermine[d] the unified effort on [each] individual campus."

"It is our hope," Dean Altvater's covering letter declared, "that the matter may be handled in such a way as to avoid any unnecessary publicity and any appearance of censure of North Carolina citizens who may have supported the Symphony in good faith."

A copy of Dean Altvater's letter and statement was sent to me by Chancellor Robert B. House, along with this note:

Ben,

You gave a good account of yourself [at the meeting] yesterday.

I hope this impasse can be dissolved so that you can get on with your great idea. If this document can help you spot some possible dangers to avoid, it could be a good thing.

At any rate, I want you to have a copy.

Cordially yours,
RBH

I remain puzzled to this day by the opposition offered to the Symphony by a few academics. My proposal in 1937 to merge the University Orchestra with the WPA musicians was an eminently logical one, which could have benefited music education directly in the classroom and indirectly in the concert hall. There is little doubt that if given the opportunity, several musicians from the WPA orchestra could have become excellent teacher-scholars at the University while doing valuable work in the University Orchestra. Surely the weaknesses of that group pointed to the need for experienced players.

But Dr. Glen Haydon objected to allowing credits for performance on the basis that what North Carolina needed was musicians with a broad general education. The emphasis in the music department was on academic pursuits, specifically musicology. I too favored a "broad general education" rather than a limited, specialized, "conservatory" training. But I believed that performance training for talented students could, and should, be provided, just as the University of Indiana and the University of Michigan have done successfully.

Fortunately, I was not the only one who was puzzled and dismayed by Dean Altvater's letter in 1944. A flurry of letters ensued, and the University administration expressed its concern. Negotiations took place. By early 1945 procedures had been worked out to ensure that Symphony participation would not interfere with students' responsibilities to their colleges (formalizing the precautions that we had observed all along).

Meanwhile, music students were being attracted to our new organization. But unhappily the prejudice against us was unrelenting, and the opposition of several music department heads, along with others unsympathetic to the aims and progress of the new Symphony, was still evident.

"That orchestra is not needed," they insisted, "because our own institutions can provide all the music required for the state."

Although there were few opportunities for an open confrontation, there were occasions when the orchestra was denied the use of institutional facilities—such as a hall in which to rehearse, or even music stands or chairs. And there was a persistent effort to have me dismissed from the University's music department. Further, two University officials later told me that on three different occasions during my ten years of teaching there, I had been recommended for promotion to a full professorship—but because of my work with the Symphony and at the insistence of one individual on the faculty committee, my promotion had been denied.

Why is it that when a new idea develops and is being brought to fruition—I have pondered this through the years and the answer still eludes me—opposition crystallizes and seeks to make a project one of the seven deadly sins?

One of the finest compliments I have ever been given—surely the most treasured—I share with Professor Albert M. Coates, founder and director of the nationally recognized North Carolina Institute of Government. Chancellor House was chatting one day with Chapel Hill friends when our names were mentioned.

"Albert Coates and Ben Swalin are the two nuts on the Carolina campus," Bob House told them, "because from their small acorns great oaks will grow."

T H E small acorn of the North Carolina Symphony Orchestra did not spring forth from the fertile soil of Tarheelia into quick fruition, however. As time went on it proved its value with its educational services and musical programs, and wherever the players went, the people took them to their hearts. The project grew in spite of harassment, and we were privileged to return year after year to the same communities and also to extend our tours. But it was an uphill road.

Because our players were then volunteers, they frequently had scheduling conflicts. I could never be sure how many musicians would actually be on stage for any concert. I felt strongly that we needed to upgrade our organization in order to keep the orchestra alive and growing, and the guiding spirits of the Symphony Society agreed. In late 1944, therefore, plans were developed for an expansion program. We hoped to raise $150,000, so as to be able to engage forty full-time musicians for the orchestra in addition to musicians located geographically within reach, thereby making it possible for us to play twenty or thirty concerts and also to develop the Children's Concert Division (see Chapter 7). By "full-time musician" we meant one available on some reasonable basis, firmed up by a contract for the season.

Paul Green graciously accepted the chairmanship of the project. "I'll take the job," he promised characteristically, "in case you can't get anybody else." Of course we couldn't get anybody else. If I remember correctly, we didn't try.

We felt that professional fund-raising assistance would be a wise investment, and the Society contracted with the American City Bureau of Chicago. Kenneth Sickler, a southerner employed by that agency, arrived from Chicago to study the project.

"The Symphony's problem is not fund-raising," he concluded after a careful appraisal of the situation, "it is creating an informed public. The Symphony is capable of selling itself."

Unfortunately, our expansion drive opened in December 1944, precisely as the disastrous "Battle of the Bulge" was developing, and it appeared that the American forces might be pushed into the sea. The fund-raising had to be abandoned. Governor Broughton, Paul Green, Senator H. P. Taylor, and others were concerned at the turn of world events. Furthermore, it seemed that the professional fund-raising organization knew less about our problems than we did. Governor Broughton, who was familiar with the fund-raising contract, felt that very little had been accomplished and that it would be difficult to borrow money to continue with the program. Senator

Taylor advised that we should discontinue with the bureau and conclude our project in April. "This is an educational thing," he said, "and it will take some time to work up enthusiasm and interest."

Others were reluctant to surrender their hopes. Because plans for the campaign had already been made, I encouraged the group to utilize whatever motivation remained. Governor Broughton then suggested that we "borrow" a man from an institution who could head up a drive.

A committee was formed: Governor Broughton, the Society's President Harry Comer, Senator H. P. Taylor, Sr., Col. R. L. McMillan, and Benjamin Swalin. Our assignment was to designate a man to head up a drive by February 1945.

In line with Governor Broughton's suggestion that we borrow a man from one of the other state organizations or agencies to organize our revived expansion drive, Paul Green was able to obtain a leave of absence for Professor J. O. Bailey, of the University of North Carolina's English department, and Colonel McMillan accepted the chairmanship of the new drive.

We set up headquarters in a small room on North Columbia Street in Chapel Hill at the rear of a grocery store. The office equipment consisted of a few inherited tables and chairs, a "gel" machine, and a typewriter on which Dr. Bailey pecked out his letters with his index fingers. Water for our coffee and bathroom accommodations were supplied at the nearby Chapel Hill town hall. During the cold weather we were warmed by our own labors and by stoking a coal stove.

Dr. Bailey was an indefatigable worker, and during his half-year leave of absence he gave effective and aggressive leadership in the successfully developing campaign.

The drive was developed on a statewide, cooperative basis with a chairman in each of twelve districts, and quotas were set for all districts. The funds to be raised were in addition to, and separate from, the Symphony Society memberships that earned concert appearances by the orchestra.

By then, fortunately, I was able to devote my full time to the project. After ten years of teaching at the University, I was granted a leave of absence by President Graham to "build a permanent symphony orchestra, and to ascertain if it could succeed."

One of my ideas that year for spreading the message of the Symphony was to record one or more "Pops" albums of American compositions and selections for children. Hoping that our nonprofit Symphony might be granted a lower recording fee, I tried to enlist the aid of the national office of the American Federation of Musicians, which by virtue of its authority over musical personnel controlled the price structures of all union recording sessions. However, this was during the Petrillo controversy with President Franklin D. Roosevelt, and, in my desire to utilize technological advantages for the benefit of the people, I suddenly found myself in the middle of the controversy.

James C. Petrillo, at that time president of the American Federation of Musicians, was using his power to block the making of any recordings for use by radio stations on the grounds that such use deprived union musicians of their livelihood. If a radio station were to broadcast recordings, it would have no need to maintain its own orchestra. As someone who had played in such an orchestra, I could certainly understand that side of the issue, as could many others. But Petrillo's success in controlling the music industry made for him many enemies and produced much litigation.

I was brought into the arena after one of our Symphony board members on his own initiative, and with good intentions, while visiting in New York tried to facilitate union negotiations—but with unfortunate results. An already sensitive situation became extremely difficult. A reduction in the recording fees was flatly denied us, and I had to cancel the project. We simply could not afford to make the recordings.

Not long thereafter I was in Asheville for a morning rehearsal at a local high school, and I was summoned to answer a long-distance telephone call. An unidentified man in New York told me he was a representative of the American Federation of Musicians. "I've been told that you are blocking the recording project," he said. "Now I hate to do this to you, because I know you are a nice fellow. But since the union's strike against the government and President Roosevelt is still continuing, I will be forced to publicize your anti-union attitude."

"I've had nothing whatsoever to do with the union strike," I answered warmly. "And I've been a member of the New York Union's Local No. 802 since 1921. It's unfair to instigate adverse publicity against us!"

By some miracle, the next morning's newspapers announced that the strike had been settled. And I never heard another word from the unidentified "representative."

T H O S E were busy months for Maxine and me. When we were not working in the office, we were crisscrossing North Carolina playing joint violin and piano programs and addressing public meetings to raise funds for the orchestra's projected first statewide tour.

Soon after agreeing to accept the responsibility for the Symphony fund drive, Dr. Bailey wrote Harry Comer, then president of the Society, a two-and-a-half-page letter asking for answers to an array of questions. He wanted to know, for example:

> What kind of musical services do we offer in places such as Valdese, West Jefferson, Burgaw? Can their members of the Symphony Fund attend concerts fifty miles away? . . .
>
> General membership of $1 with a twenty-cent tax at the door seems acceptable to the people; but to what are they entitled? Is the membership valid anywhere? In a different district? . . .
>
> How much lower is the guarantee for programs if the community raises its quota for the Symphony Fund? . . .
>
> Can workers approach the same person twice? Is the Symphony Fund contribution good for an extended period? . . .
>
> Barnum and Bailey found it expensive to parade, but it was worth the money and trouble. Are children's concerts our "parade" and talking point? . . .

If the orchestra plays in Camp Lejeune, the people in Jacksonville ask, "Why can't a dozen players come to Jacksonville and play free over the weekend?" Or why not come to Oxford Orphanage and play on Saturday morning "when the musicians are not busy"? . . .

With only one-seventh of North Carolinians [living] in cities, we should deliver the music to the right places!

In our traveling over North Carolina, Maxine and I found ourselves confronted with many of the same questions that Dr. Bailey encountered, but we were glad to see that such troublesome issues were being resolved and that contributions and memberships were taking on a clearer image.

By the end of Dr. Bailey's leave of absence from the University, our joint efforts had raised $65,000. We were determined to press our campaign further, and we persuaded the Symphony board that it was essential to have a business manager. Fortunately for us, Col. Kermit Hunter obtained his release from the armed forces and agreed to accept the responsibility here. He began his duties with us on September 10, 1945, applying his considerable talents between the Symphony office and the various districts where chairmen were in the process of raising their quotas for our initial orchestra tour.

Two months after Kermit Hunter took over the business management of the orchestra we were engaged to play four concerts at Camp Lejeune, the big Marine base at Jacksonville, North Carolina. We were to give a performance for adults, two children's concerts, and a special program at the base hospital for war casualties over the two-day period of November 17–18, 1945, and we were being paid a fee of $3,350 for our services.

We were in good spirits as we worked to prepare for the Camp Lejeune tour. We looked forward eagerly to the engagement, but a little fearfully, too. How many players would show up in time for the first concert? We wondered. How many might find themselves stranded by engine trouble or flat tires or—the mere contemplation gave us shudders—a serious accident?

Maxine and I arrive at Camp Lejeune (1945)

Typical of our uncertainty is a report I made to Kermit Hunter: "Thus far, for the Camp Lejeune concerts there are: Definite, eighteen women and thirty men—This includes you and me! Indefinite, three women and three men."

On our arrival at Camp Lejeune, we were treated to a regal dinner before the evening concert, and there were refreshments after the concert. But even more memorable was the next morning's breakfast: for the first time in many months, we enjoyed bacon, ham, and eggs! The Marines enjoyed our visit too. When we were playing Grofé's *Grand Canyon Suite* and reached the part that was at that time providing the musical theme of a popular cigarette advertisement, one of the enthusiastically approving Marines jumped to his feet and yelled, "Call for Philip Mor-ris-s-s!"

For the weekend of hospitality and the joy of communicating through music, we cleared $960.55. But there had been a note of sadness, too. Among the guests at the concert were friends from New Jersey, Dr. and Mrs. Berthold T. D. Schwarz, whose son Eric, a double bassist in our orchestra, had been killed in the war; another double bassist, George Haley of Asheville, had lost his life at the battle of Guadalcanal, and memorial memberships were given to commemorate these fine young soldiers and artists.

I n addressing the Symphony Society's annual meeting in the fall of 1945 I emphasized the continued pressing need for developing the orchestra and outlined what I felt were the most important reasons for this. The first problem confronting us, and perhaps the most difficult of solution, concerned those of our musicians who had families and home responsibilities. For them, there were frequent unavoidable conflicts of interest at home or school, and sometimes a concert might have one less player.

Another problem was that of musicians with full-time positions, or the musician-coach who could not rehearse or play in concerts on weekends during the football or basketball seasons.

The scarcity of capable string players was also troubling, and it demonstrated the need for more good music teachers in order to develop string players able to perform acceptably.

The logistics surely were not favorable for moving an indeterminate—but considerable—number of men and women over many miles, and for providing lodging and meals when the engagement was overnight. That we were able to do it was because the musicians loved to make music and to play together: no formal contracts required their attending rehearsals and performing the concerts. And somehow, the last-minute problems were usually solved. If one player could not make it to a concert, another member of the orchestra might switch instrumental parts and play the missing part.

The musicians were determined to develop and maintain an exemplary symphony orchestra of which they, as well as other friends of the fine arts in North Carolina, could be proud. Had they been less willing to contribute their time, their energies, their expense monies, and, most importantly, their abiding and abounding faith in our project, the North Carolina Symphony would have died away quickly to silence.

CHAPTER 5

On Tour at Last!

OUR ambition to take our orchestra to the people of North Carolina was happily fulfilled in the spring of 1946, when our successful fund-raising drive enabled us to go on tour to some 50 communities to play 104 concerts—including 50 free children's programs!

This was a new and wonderful experience! For the first time, we were a professional "Orchestra on Wheels," traveling as a group in our own chartered buses for three months of concertizing. We had to leave our comfortable home life behind; but we were able to develop a real sense of community as we rolled across the state and experienced together the vicissitudes of hotel-living and restaurant-eating.

For our first season of touring we devised a pattern that remained in effect until the late 1960s: in the first part of the season (February and March) the Little Symphony of approximately twenty-five players toured the smaller communities of the state; these players were then joined by roughly thirty others to form the full Symphony, which toured the larger towns in April and early May. In this way we were able to utilize the services of musicians from larger professional orchestras, who could join us after their regular seasons were over. And the Little Symphony was able to bring music to communities that lacked an auditorium of sufficient size to accommodate a full orchestra.

We were privileged to perform for thousands of North Carolinians representing this state's wealth of diverse and yet essentially

37

similar cultures. Down in coastal Hyde County we listened entranced as they called their county "Hoyde" and referred to the hours when the "toydes" would be "hoygh" and low. And all over the mountain counties we loved the smooth, flat gliding of their long vowels and diphthongs when they saw the "b-u-us" and complimented the orchestra's "r-i-ight n-i-ice" playing.

That year brought the orchestra many dividends in experiences shared, new friends and supporters acquired and appreciated. We learned first-hand the journalist's evaluation of his profession: "You don't make much money, but you meet such interesting people."

I remember particularly a lady we met one night early on the tour. The orchestra was quartered in an old-fashioned hotel-inn with a commodious lobby where we relaxed after the concert. This dear lady owned the hostelry, and she was eager and ready whenever an opportunity was presented to lead everyone into conversation about MUSIC! She had attended the concert and had liked it, and she wanted everyone to know it. "I like all music that sounds like a bell," she declared. *Tales of the Vienna Woods* had been on the program, so we presumed that the bird calls had rung a bell for her!

W I T H the start of our tour that spring, it became apparent that we needed to have someone on duty at the office while we were away. So for the first time we employed a full-time secretary. Although she had been trained for office duties, visions of her impending marriage and her appointments at the beauty parlor were sometimes in conflict with her secretarial work. This was suggested when I would call the office on the telephone and get no answer. To other callers, I feared, it would indicate that the office was no longer open for business. So whenever possible, I would return to the office to check on the correspondence, dictate outgoing letters, and perhaps look over carbons of letters I had earlier dictated.

One day I picked up the copy of a letter addressed to J. Spencer Love, at that time president of Burlington Mills and one of the nation's leaders in the textile industry, who was generous in his support of civic causes and educational and artistic enterprises. I had dictated the letter over the telephone to our secretary, but hadn't seen it before it was mailed to Mr. Love—a risky procedure, I discovered. My letter's opening sentence was meant to be an apology to Mr. Love for my having been belated in replying to a letter he had written to me. But that was hardly what I had said, according to our secretary. Imagine my surprise and chagrin when I picked up the carbon and read: "Dear Mr. Love: I have been somewhat *benevolent* in answering your letter. . . ."

Our sometimes starry-eyed secretary's unique choice of words must have amused Spencer Love. If it irritated him in any sense, he never indicated it to us. He would remain, all his life, one of the Symphony's staunch friends and *benevolent* supporters.

T H E North Carolina Symphony Society met on May 19, 1946, and elected a new president—Spencer Murphy of Salisbury, one of North Carolina's prominent supporters of the arts. After his graduation in 1925 with the bachelor of arts degree from the University at Chapel Hill, where he earned distinction for his work on the staffs of the various student publications, Spencer had returned to Salisbury to launch a distinguished career in journalism with the *Salisbury Post*, of which he became editor. His popularity, and particularly the regard his fellow journalists had for him, served well the Society's efforts to strengthen the orchestra. There was another factor, too, that helped our cause: Spencer was Pete Murphy's son. Walter Murphy, known affectionately across the state as Pete Murphy, was for years one of North Carolina's regularly elected political leaders. He served several terms in the North Carolina General Assembly during which he was speaker of the House of Representatives.

At this May meeting another able and faithful protagonist of the arts—author, journalist, and educator Dr. Sylvester Green—made a motion (seconded by Dr. Christopher C. Crittenden, director of the North Carolina Historical Commission): "That the authority for total administration of both the Orchestra and the Society be vested in one man, to be known as the Director of the Society, with the

The Symphony comes to Macon County
(Courtesy of the North Carolina Department of Archives and History)

understanding that he may designate or secure others as assistant directors, and with the duties of each specifically stated." The motion passed, and I was named to that post.

With my election as director of the orchestra and the Society, "consistent with such policies as are prescribed by the executive committee," a special committee made up of three members of the executive committee was designated to assist in obtaining the needed personnel.

My appointment as director conveyed to the orchestra a single line of authority and avoided the *Sturm und Drang* of business contra music. It served us well, as the records reveal. It was essential not only that we create a blueprint of service and musical enlightenment and inspiration, but also that we accomplish tasks outside the area of musical performance. Especially burdensome were our fiscal responsibilities, and the challenge of encouraging and promoting the statewide membership campaign that continues even today.

I N the fall of our first statewide tour season of 1946, we appeared before the Advisory Budget Commission of the General Assembly with an appeal for an appropriation of $15,000. We pointed out that our tour had included fifty free performances for school children in accordance with our principle that the Symphony was an educational institution, and that a pattern had been set for the operations of the Symphony chapters whereby each community that attained its full membership quota received, in addition to an evening concert for its members, one admission-free program for the school children of the community. (Sometimes, but not often, we would hear opposition expressed to our providing free children's concerts. In Winston-Salem, for example, some individuals opposed the presentation of any free concerts for the children on the basis that such action was "socialistic." Nevertheless, we resolutely maintained the principle of admission-free matinees in spite of the urgent need for additional supporting funds.)

As a new touring orchestra in 1946 we had also begun our Young Adult Auditions project. The purpose of these auditions was to give those with exceptional talent the opportunity to launch their careers by performing to professional standards—another aspect of our educational role. The system that we developed was as follows: Once each year we would bring together panels of from three to six eminent performers and teachers of music to judge the applicants in three categories: instrumentalists aged seventeen or older; vocalists aged seventeen or older; and junior instrumentalists, aged sixteen or younger. Instrumentalists were judged by instrumentalists, and vocalists by vocalists. The panels were instructed to vote by ballot for a winner and a runner-up and to count the ballots *before* they consulted with each other. Our staff and I would listen to the auditions, but we never participated in the voting or discussions.

The music played by the applicants was to be selected from a list circulated well in advance of the auditions. Each performance was to be judged on both its technical and its aesthetic merits. The number of winners each year varied with the number and skill of the applicants, as did the number of concerts in which each winner performed. Adult winners performed in adult concerts and received honoraria for their performances. Junior soloists were featured in children's concerts without honorarium.

During the orchestra's twenty-five touring years between 1947 and 1972, it was our privilege to present 110 soloists selected from annual auditions. Several junior and adult soloists were invited to return because they had endeared themselves to the public and proved their exceptional ability.

Among our talented child soloists who have gone on to distinguish themselves as outstanding pianists are Yoko Nozaki, of Durham (now Mrs. Emanuel Ax); Jayne Winfield, of Washington, N.C. (Mrs. Daniel Ericourt); Nancy L. Lassiter, of Smithfield (Mrs. Nancy L. Huggin), who joined the business staff of the Metropolitan Opera; Michael Ponti, of Fort Bragg (now a recording artist in Berlin); Bobby Morris, of Atlantic; Joan Melton, of Albemarle; and Caroline Corbett Taylor, of Wadesboro (the granddaughter of Senator H. P. Taylor). Commendably, these youthful talents were coached in their piano concertos by their local teachers.

The adult audition soloists whom I recall particularly include Bert Adams, baritone, Chapel Hill; Marilyn Burris, soprano, Greensboro; Paul Hickfang, bass-baritone, Greenville; Carolyn Smith Morgan, pianist, Greensboro; Sophia Steffan, mezzo soprano, High Point; Wayne Turnage, baritone, Dunn, who later joined the San Francisco Opera; Betty Honeycutt Williams, soprano, Concord; Marilyn Zschau, mezzo soprano, Greensboro, later with the New York City Opera and the Metropolitan Opera; and Nicholas Zumbro, pianist, and John Thurman, 'cellist, both of New York. Their talent and schooling merited our faith in their extraordinary abilities.

W E opened our second season of statewide touring by performing a special concert on February 17, 1947, before the members of the North Carolina General Assembly at the State Capitol. It was the first time, we were told, that a symphony orchestra had "invaded" the premises of an American state legislature to petition for a regular state appropriation. That year the General Assembly had increased its allocation to the North Carolina Symphony to $24,000 for the biennium, and we wished to thank the legislators with a musical tribute.

Our traveling repertoire for the second tour was extensive and ambitious. It comprised fifty works, including four symphonies; nine concertos for piano, violin, viola, 'cello, flute, and harp; and arias for three vocalists. Larger audiences were also reached through fifteen radio broadcasts. At the close of the second annual membership drive in 1947, forty-nine of the state's one hundred counties had established Symphony Society chapters.

We were on the move. The North Carolina Symphony Orchestra was becoming a fact of life. "This Is Your Music" was becoming our new motto.

Although most subscribers to symphony orchestras in the United States are concentrated in city areas, our 11,500 Symphony Society members in 1947 were representative primarily of rural communities with merely a few larger cities. We knew that these members were potentially "listening musicians" and, as Howard Hanson once aptly phrased it, "It is just as important to have one million listeners as it is to have one thousand good professionals." *The New Republic* in August of that year, in reviewing our project, wrote that we refused to admit that any community anywhere could fail to appreciate good music.

A month later, in September 1947, John Temple Graves in his syndicated column wrote a lyrical review entitled "North Carolina's Music," praising our efforts and achievements:

> When music, heavenly maid, was young,
> Where first in early Greece she sung. . . .

When music was really young it was not what our young people today are persuaded it is. It included no sex call of the lower animals, no savage tom-toms of one-one-one, no synthetic animations of tired pretenders, no improvisation by awful incompetents, no offerings by vulgarians who lead bands and think what they like is what the public likes, and no mere childish noise makings. It was more like what the North Carolina Symphony Orchestra has played this season to some 100,000 children and 50,000 adults of that enlightened state in smallest towns and largest cities, in a 3,600-mile tour with 114 appearances. This remarkable organization is proving . . . it is a people's orchestra in every sense of the word. It is made up of players who come from many walks and ways. It plays to people of all walks and ways. . . . It is supported in part by the people direct and in part by the state of North Carolina. It is the first orchestra in America to receive state support. It opened its season this year with a concert in the state capitol before a joint session of the legislature.

It is even more deeply a people's orchestra in that it's proving things about people, and bringing out things in people, letting it come about that the so-called common man is not so common as some of those who cater to him would have it.

In keeping with the aim of developing an orchestra capable of bringing fine music to the people, we had the responsibility for engaging proficient players of good character. And leadership had to be provided for each section: strings, woodwinds, brasses, and percussion. When such leadership was not available from within the state, we had to look elsewhere; for we were obligated to project a season of concerts and a tour with the knowledge that the players would be available for every concert, and be competent musically, as well as reliable. A *few* volunteer players were also employed *occasionally* for special concerts, or to provide replacements when needed—but the North Carolina Symphony was almost from the beginning of its state-supported life an orchestra of approximately 55 or 60 regular players under union contracts.

Music on a Shoestring

FROM our beginning days the orchestra was blessed in having behind it a strongly supportive Symphony Society. We were fortunate also in having sound business leadership. And that was essential if we were to produce and survive. A dollar in those days loomed large. Dollars were hard to come by, and we had to make them stretch a long way. And usually they did. One of our firm principles was to avoid running up a large deficit.

Albin Pikutis was one of our ablest "dollar-stretchers." Albin had been with the newly organized orchestra since its revival. He had been one of my finest violin students, and he was an excellent musician. With Maxine, he had provided stalwart support in getting our orchestra rejuvenated. His appointment as business manager and assistant treasurer of the Symphony Society proved to be a very "sound" investment.

At the annual meeting of the society on July 1, 1948, the minutes reveal, Albin's salary was set at $3,600. At that same meeting my salary was increased to $6,000 annually, and Maxine's to $1,500. Honoraria of $100 were listed to Adeline McCall for her "Symphony Stories" (see Chapter 7) and to A. C. Hall as treasurer. All staff members traveling on Symphony business were to receive six cents per mile for the use of their automobiles.

Today, the supporters of the Symphony—and even we ourselves —wonder how we managed to get along as well as we did and to have an apparent impact upon North Carolina culture. But then we

Attentive children in Franklin, N.C.

recall that in those days one could go into a grocery store and buy a loaf of bread for five cents, or a chocolate bar, or chewing gum, and one could drop a nickel into a Coke machine and have a soft-drink bottle fall out; and even in Chapel Hill it was possible to rent a house or an apartment for $50 a month or less.

CRUCIAL to our financial survival was the level of success we had with our various local Symphony chapters. The thermometer readings on those success charts ranged all the way from almost zero to normal, and occasionally to fever pitch.

The initial impetus for the formation of a new chapter most often came from the hard work of our field representative, who would arrange to meet with local women's clubs and businessmen's associations in order to bring them the message of the Symphony. In the early days, when we were first reviving the Symphony and our staff was small, Maxine and I were the ones who toured the state looking for supporters. Once we had become a professional orchestra we were glad to have a staff member doing that work for us. But sometimes the standard procedures for obtaining a chapter's support would not be productive. On such occasions, if Maxine could interrupt her other activities, she would be sent on a trouble-shooting mission to that community—and she was almost always successful.

One night Maxine returned home late from a problem town, where a meeting had been called to set up an organization of new officers and workers. She reported that the sparsely attended session hadn't gone well and she had feared that she would fail to arouse the local citizens from their lethargy. But then an attractive little blonde lady who had been urged to serve as the next drive chairman hopped up from her chair: "The last thing my husband said to me before I left home," she declared, "was 'Don't get mixed up in any entanglin' alliances.'"

Maxine stood up. "I agree with her," she told the group. "The Symphony's appearance in this community might be an 'entangling alliance' because it will be an *extra* for the schools to purchase recordings relating to the children's programs, and for the teachers to attend the Symphony's area workshops as well as to teach the music to the children. It might also be an *extra* for the principals to arrange for the children to ride in buses for the concert, which will be free to them although adults will be required to pay for memberships." The result—a lady, eyes shining, waved her hand. "I'll be chairman," she said. The others signed the list as workers, and the chapter's support of the orchestra's return was assured.

As I recall the subsequent work of that chapter and its chairman, I think also of other outstanding membership chairmen whose able and faithful leadership contributed immeasurably to the success of our Symphony. Two stand out particularly: Mrs. G. Earl Davis and L. C. Gifford of Hickory, who for twenty-three consecutive years successfully undertook leadership of their local chapter.

W I T H the continuing growth of the Symphony's supporting chapters, the membership files of the office were expanding over a large portion of the Swain Hall balcony area that had been partially restructured for our use. Russell Grumman, director of the University's Extension Division and a valued supporter of the Symphony (he later served as president of the Society), had generously arranged for the Symphony to have its headquarters in a heated building and to become a constituent of campus life. Swain Hall had been built as an eating commons (thus becoming known to generations of students as "Swine" Hall), and it had subsequently been used for sundry other purposes. During our regime, a varied assortment of organizations were housed in partitioned areas around the balconies that in other times had looked down upon hundreds of students eating or, at Commencement and other gala occasions, dancing to the music of "name" bands.

From our elevated vantage point on the hot balcony we had a full view of the budding Television and Radio department on the opposite balcony. One of our other notable neighbors in Swain Hall was Norman Cordon, a former Metropolitan Opera basso, who had come home to North Carolina to help stimulate interest in music and the arts. Norman's office was a ten-by-twelve foot area by a side entrance, and sometimes on windy days you might see his corre-

spondence scattered to the hallway and stairs. But whether correspondence was mislaid, or lost, or gone blowing with the wind,
affairs could be settled usually on football Saturdays when everyone
else in Chapel Hill was at Kenan Stadium.

The staff worked hard and faithfully in our stuffed balcony head-
quarters. In 1947 our team consisted of: Albin Pikutis, business
manager; Collins Ervin, field representative; Eve Fuller, secretary;
Dorothy Elliott, publicity; Helene Grimes, membership secretary;
Adeline McCall, who gave able direction to the Children's Concert
Division; and the Swalins.

We had been anticipating with apprehension the first formidable
deficit for the Symphony's program. During a football game in
1949 I met with J. Spencer Love, our civic-minded friend, and
discussed with him our seemingly precarious position; the result
was a munificent gift to the Symphony Society of $10,000. Of even
more satisfaction to us, that contribution became the first in a series
of gifts coming to us from communities in North Carolina in which
Burlington plants were located. This generous gift also encouraged
and stimulated other large corporations and enterprises to adopt a
new open-handed policy in dealing with our requests for financial
assistance.

By 1950 the Society had approximately 20,000 members. The
establishment of additional chapters meant increased work in maintaining them, which required field work by the administrative staff.
Often we would attend a chapter banquet centered on local talent.
Other times we had occasion to speak and stress the important role
of the arts.

T H E Symphony chapters generally were sustained on a year-round
basis by supportive friends who served as chapter officers. They
were the architects of the chapter's vitality in a community. Outstanding in such efforts to develop and sustain local interest in the
Symphony's growing success was the chapter at Asheville, where
Mrs. Charles E. Dameron was the experienced and gifted entrepre-
neur of banquets given annually by the James G. K. McClure Foundation for guests from Asheville and western North Carolina.

Maxine and I remember those inspiring occasions in Asheville, which were happily anticipated by Symphony Society members from small and rural communities as far west as Franklin, northward to Spruce Pine, and southward toward the South Carolina mountains. These banquets, held in one of the large hotel ballrooms, promoted good will within the chapters and stimulated them to renewed efforts. Everybody knew that following the delicious dinner an enjoyable concert would more than compensate for the difficulties of hard mountain traveling. But even more important than the fellowship, the entertainment, or the food was the opportunity for the leaders of city and county schools to testify to the value of their 9,000 school children being able to hear and participate in the Symphony's special matinees. I also enjoyed the honor of addressing the guests at these auspicious events.

Another active and loyal supporter in Asheville was Joseph De-Nardo, who had tried so hard to hold the WPA orchestra together. He was an extremely generous man, as well as a fine musician, and he was always cooperative in sustaining our new developments. His daughter May Jo (Mrs. Gregory Perky) was a great talent on both violin and piano; she was truly a versatile performer. She served as first-chair violinist during our early tours, and she was also featured as a piano soloist in several performances of the Grieg *Piano Concerto*. May Jo, who graduated from the UNC music department, was one of my most gifted students.

Asheville, indeed, provided us lavishly with appreciation, assistance, and talent. Its audiences were among the finest in the state, and we looked forward to returning there each new season.

CHAPTER 7

Reaching Young Ears

I T was largely on the basis of our educational program for children that we had approached the General Assembly for funding in 1943. From the beginning, the officers of the Symphony Society were in agreement that there should be no charge on an individual basis, regardless of the nature of local sponsorship, for the admission of children to our school matinees.

My interest in exposing children to the cultural arts dates back at least as far as the years 1919 and 1920, when as a young violinist in the Minneapolis Symphony I participated in the orchestra's programs for children under the German conductor Emil Oberhoffer. I shall be grateful always for the training I received under his baton, and particularly for his interest in presenting outstanding children's concerts.

In 1934, the year after Oberhoffer's death, while I was visiting a Moscow Park of Culture and Rest I was impressed by a group of professional actors who performed for young Russian audiences with a repertoire from the classics and new plays. Eight years later in North Carolina, in 1942, we began to invite children to rehearsals to hear the instruments demonstrated and to ask questions. The genuine curiosity and interest shown by these children heightened our own interest and strengthened our determination to plan an educational program tailored to the needs of children, especially those living in the more rural areas, where some of the schools had no music teachers. Usually the parents of the children supported our endeavors to introduce their offspring to the delights of good music. But occasionally our kind of music was not to the parents' liking because they preferred "hillbilly" music and thought their children would too.

Many of the children did like—as did we—the picking and singing kind of music, but we were happy to discover, as we advanced in our children's program, that they also enjoyed the kind we were bringing them. In developing concerts of music especially appropriate for the young, we had the good fortune to gain the friendship and support of Mrs. Fred B. McCall of the public schools in Chapel Hill. Mrs. McCall was an excellent musician with authoritative standards of music for youthful audiences. Her guidance was an important factor in the success of the program.

Adeline Denham McCall had come to live with the Koch family —Mrs. Frederick H. Koch was her aunt—and to enroll as a student in the University. From her first days in Chapel Hill, she was one of the Carolina Playmakers' most enthusiastic, hardest-working, and most popular members. When Maxine and I arrived in Chapel Hill, Adeline had graduated from the University, had studied at the Peabody Conservatory and in New York, and had become the wife of Professor Fred B. McCall of the University's school of law (who was a capable tympanist). The McCalls were among the first of the faculty folk we met, and from that happy day Adeline has been one of the Symphony's devoted coworkers and friends.

The Children's Concert Division of the North Carolina Symphony was organized in 1945 with Adeline McCall as educational director and Maxine Swalin as coordinator for the Symphony and the elementary schools. The programs of music education were developed through cooperation with the public schools, based on the knowledge that children can assimilate through visual, aural, and kinetic means. Several months in advance of each new season, our three-way team—Adeline, Maxine, and I—planned two programs: one for the Little Symphony and another for the Full Symphony. Mrs. McCall's expertise was significant not only in selecting music appropriate for children in the grades, but also in assembling mate-

Adeline McCall at work
(Photo by Maury Faggart)

rials and recordings for the classrooms and libraries of the participating schools.

The programs were planned to last just under an hour, and to include variety and contrast. Typically, there would be a suite or a symphony (abbreviated, if necessary, to capture and sustain the children's attention), rhythmic dances, descriptive or dramatic music, and a comic or entertaining selection. There would be two songs for all to sing (generally, a hymn and a folk song), and we encouraged them to play their melody and rhythm instruments along with the orchestra in one of the songs.

The impact of the concert was generated by weeks of preparation in the classroom. An important guide for the teachers and children was the "Symphony Stories" that Adeline McCall compiled each year. In these booklets the children could learn about the music and the composers' lives; they were given the words and music for the "Everybody Sings" portion of the concert; and there might be a cartoon, a quiz, and even rules for polite listening in the booklet.

To help them get "the feel" of music, children often danced with free creative movement while listening to a recording of one of the program selections, or they might play percussion instruments to a symphonic movement as an experience in note reading.

To make sure that *everyone* would profit from our visits, Mrs. McCall prepared a "Guide for Teachers" for each program, and in 1954 she inaugurated a series of teachers' workshops. First in Chapel Hill, and then in various locations across the state, she demonstrated the techniques that she had developed in the Chapel Hill public schools. The teachers then returned to their home communities with new enthusiasm for communicating music to their pupils.

"SYMPHONY DAY" was usually an auspicious occasion in the schools, and the host community generally welcomed the Symphony with banners and signs lavishly displayed. Exhibited in the hallways were children's paintings and other things made by them, such as toy musical instruments done with remarkable precision. At Elizabethtown, I recall, there was a welcoming committee with Cub Scouts in command, and when the orchestra bus drove up behind the schoolhouse, they shouted a well-rehearsed welcoming cheer. They were thrilled to be permitted to carry the instruments to the stage, and particularly to lift the big drums. As the women of the orchestra entered the school building, Girl Scouts stationed along the hall escorted them to the lounge and to the "green room," the proud temporary designation of their home economics room (Maxine was asked by a third-grade escort if she would like to go to the "Lingerie room"). After the morning concert we were treated to an excellent lunch prepared by the home economics students.

But Symphony Day in the schools, especially during wet and snowy weather, sometimes presented problems. One wise principal in a mountain county, anticipating the mess that tracked-in mud would make on his new gymnasium floor, had the children bring sheets of newspapers to spread on it before they sat down to listen to the concert.

At the conclusion of the program that day, a freckled-faced, red-haired boy was walking backward to the exit so he might get a last glimpse of his favorite instrument, the drums, when he stumbled and fell at Maxine's feet. Plainly chagrined, he scrambled up.

"I fell good," he stammered, grinning, "but I'm OK. I came jes' to get out o' school anyway. But I liked it jes' the same."

The children had not only favorite instruments, but also favorite pieces that they wanted to hear again. Until the early 1950s they were able to dictate the encore to be played at the evening concert by paying a Junior Membership fee of fifty cents, which admitted them to the adult evening concert. When they arrived at the concert they handed the usher a slip of paper naming their favorite from that season's list of possible encores. The ballots would be counted, and the "winner" would be the featured encore—much to the children's delight.

In cities throughout the state, and in consolidated school districts, children's concert audiences from one community sometimes numbered 5,000 or 6,000. At Elon College, for example, the gymnasium would accommodate 4,135 Alamance County children. The Greensboro Coliseum would seat 6,546 city children, followed by approximately the same number from the Guilford County schools.

In the more rural areas each concert would attract children from many small schools and townships, and the program narrator at the matinees (generally, this was Maxine) made a point of reading off the names of the schools participating. For example, in western North Carolina when we performed in the Andrews high school gymnasium, children came to it in school buses from Hiwassee Dam, Hanging "Dawg," Martin's Creek, Peachtree, Tomatla, Marble, Hayesville, Mt. Pleasant, Walker, and Murphy. In the coastal section of the state, performances at Beaufort or Morehead City brought together school children from Sea Level, Atlantic, Harker's Island, Smyrna, and Newport.

Boatloads of parents with children of all ages came from Ocracoke and other island settlements to a matinee performance at Cape Hatteras where the schoolroom was heated by a stove with the longest stovepipe we had ever seen. But the *hottest* stovepipe was the one in Franklin's Friendship Tabernacle. We played in the primitive sawdust-floored tabernacle in February, and the only source of heat was an old pot-bellied wood stove in the center of the room. The stovepipe went straight up to a right-angled turn near the ceiling, and along the greater part of its length it was red-hot. The musicians performed in their overcoats, but they couldn't play with their gloves on. They were more apprehensive about their delicate instruments, though, than about their stiff fingers. And we were all worried for the safety of the children and their parents and friends attending the concert with them. It was the first children's concert in Macon County, and they had come there from as far away as Highlands and Bryson City; and because there were not enough school buses to transport them, some of the children had come standing up in cattle trucks.

That Franklin concert was quite a successful occasion in every way. Nobody, children or grownups, was involved in a highway accident; no one suffered frostbite or burns. We orchestra members survived without notable damage, and so did our instruments, though the stage was perilously close to that roaring stove and the red-hot stovepipe. And the audience, particularly the children, gave us enthusiastic approval. Considering everything, we had played well. It hadn't been a routine performance presented in routine fashion—but few programs could be so designated.

"Home was never like this," said one member of the group after some trivial mishap had disturbed him. His declaration might well have become the slogan of our travelogue, it seems, as I look back on the rigors of our schedule, with a children's concert during the day often being followed by a full-scale performance for adults that evening. Such two-concert days were tiring, particularly when the performances followed a long morning's traveling, but the warm responses of our audiences refreshed us and inspired us to advance and strengthen our efforts to bring to North Carolinians young and old a taste of good music, and to cultivate in them a growing appetite for it.

S O M E of our most effective innovations were developments in our children's programs. For example, our orchestra brought to the children of the state for the first time such pieces as Leroy Anderson's "Sleigh Ride," "Typewriter," "Waltzing Cat," and other works. We even enjoyed the privilege of having the composer conduct his compositions on tour with us in the early 1950s when he was stationed at Fort Bragg.

We also featured folk arrangements such as "Johnson's Old Gray Mule," "Old Joe Clark," and "Cripple Creek," and audiences of every age seemed transported by our arrangements of "Buttons and Bows" and "Raindrops Keep Falling on My Head." Although these never displaced the true substance of more permanent music, they served to introduce North Carolina children—and often their elders—to *American* music. And this acquaintance was broadened when we played selections by MacDowell, Griffes, Stringfield, Gershwin, Guion, Grofé, Dett, Copland, Bernstein, Gould, Menotti, Deems Taylor, and others.

I recall a statement by Rudolf Ganz, a famous pianist, who once remarked that "I played before the public for twenty years before I realized that music was not only a profession but also an entertainment."

A device we sometimes employed for encouraging the children's participation in the program was a contest in which selected elementary school children tried to identify not only the folk tunes being played but also the instruments being used in playing them. The stage setting on such occasions included chairs on the stage in front of the orchestra. When the time came for the contest to begin, the children who had been selected as their grades' representatives had the distinction of sitting with the musicians facing the audience. Once, when a bassoonist played "Twinkle, Twinkle, Little Star" in a low register, only one hand went up, and a boy soprano from a small mountain community ventured his identification of the song by singing his own version with the words: "Dan'l Boone, he kilt a b'ar!" Another time, in a town down on the coast, a fourth-grader sang as his answer to the same "Twinkle, Twinkle" his offering of "Pappy holds me on his knee."

We were occasionally lucky enough to gain the assistance of famous personalities in our school programs. Once when we learned that two members of the Trapp family were at Duke Hospital for a check-up, we asked them if they would appear at a children's concert in Memorial Hall at Chapel Hill. We were delighted, of course, when they consented. Dressed in their colorful Austrian costumes, the two sisters came on stage and joined the children of the audience in the spirited singing of "Climb Every Mountain" while the orchestra provided the lively accompaniment.

The most unusual of the guests featured at our children's programs was the immensely popular ventriloquist Edgar Bergen with his celebrated puppets, Charlie McCarthy, Mortimer Snerd, and Effie Klinker. The rumor must somehow have flown over Chapel Hill that Bergen and Charlie McCarthy were to be there; for even though it was billed as a children's program, Memorial Hall on May 1, 1952, was jammed and overflowing, with police and other adults crowding into every available space in the rear.

There was no rehearsal, but at a given signal, Mr. Bergen appeared on the stage carrying Charlie on his arm. The children were incredulous: Charlie was actually talking to them! After a short while, Bergen and Charlie disappeared backstage, and then Bergen came out with Mortimer Snerd. They exchanged quips, and to

Charlie McCarthy brings Edgar Bergen to a children's concert
(Courtesy of the North Carolina Department of Archives and History)

Bergen's exaggerated disgust, the dummy revealed his amazing, un-believable ignorance. In exasperation, Bergen finally demanded, "Mortimer, how *can* you be so stupid?"

And Mortimer, being in the South at the time, answered in slow southern vernacular: "Well, Mr. Bergen, Ah works at it."

The children, the adults, and the orchestra members yelled their delight.

Effie Klinker attracted considerable attention, too. But Charlie was really *the* star of the performance, and following the concert he and Mr. Bergen came down to a podium below the stage where the children might see Charlie better and marvel at him. They could hardly believe he was not really a live human.

That whole event had an inspirational effect, and the memory of it lingers clearly, even though Edgar Bergen has passed on and Charlie McCarthy is retired and residing at the Smithsonian Institution in Washington.

Another innovation in our children's programs was the appearance on several occasions of a lass of Scottish ancestry from Flora Macdonald College. Because many North Carolinians, particularly those in the Sandhills and Cape Fear Valley areas, have a Scottish heritage of which they are properly proud, this kilt-clad girl's part on the program was enthusiastically applauded from the moment she came down the center aisle onto the stage to the lively sound of her bagpipes to transform the concert into a veritable Scottish celebration. Scottish songs on the program were lustily sung by the children, especially in such communities as Southern Pines and Pinehurst and Aberdeen, where the Highland Fling was danced by sixth-graders.

On one occasion James Fassett, a prestigious CBS commentator, joined the Little Symphony for a nationwide radio broadcast. He taped our performance in the tiny mountain community of Banner Elk (population less than four hundred) not far from towering Mount Mitchell (at 6,684 feet, the highest mountain in eastern America). Mr. Fassett was so enthusiastic about our children's concert project and so enjoyed that locality—the teachers, the children in the local orphanage, and the other townspeople, whom he found so genuine and unspoiled and attractive—that he taped several hours of preconcert conversations in addition to our program. When he edited the recordings, he found that the technicians had measured an unbelievable length of tape in recording the diphthongs and extended vowels of the mountain children.

WE were happy to observe the children's concerts expanding in every section of the state as more schools, more students, and more parents and school patrons were becoming involved. For example, each year in Asheville's 3,000-seat city auditorium we performed *three* matinee programs, which required the transporting of 198 busloads of children from the city of Asheville and Buncombe County.

Our children's concerts apparently were also encouraging related interests and activities in the cultural advancement of the communities. In some of these communities, the concert area would be vibrant with extraordinary paintings representing the children's impressions of the music. Often huge murals illustrating Grofé's *Hudson River Suite*, Copland's *Rodeo*, or Tchaikowsky's *Nutcracker* ballet decorated the classrooms and auditorium. Exhibits such as those in Sparta and Lexington, because of their quality, reminded me of some of the children's paintings in the classes of the famed Professor Cizek in Vienna, who was proud that the paintings by his "children," as he spoke of his students, had been selected for the opening exhibition of a California museum of art.

It has been the good fortune of the North Carolina Symphony Society to enjoy a happy relationship with the public. So responsive was it to our efforts to take good music to the people that sometimes at the conclusion of our touring, our total intake of decibels had been almost exhausting. When Shakespeare wrote about music, he had in mind the "concordance of sweet sounds"—but to us, following an arduous tour, the music might have become tiresome rather than an "adventure of the spirit."

With the frequent repetition of the children's programs, one for the Little Symphony and another for the Full Orchestra, the music did at times tend to become a bit monotonous through the long, intensive seasons. At the final children's concert one season, a flutist very well expressed our feelings: "There must be something wrong with me. I'm beginning to *like* the *Blue Danube Waltz*." Nevertheless, with the occasional exception of a child soloist's playing of a concerto movement, the programs remained intact, true to the listings in Adeline McCall's "Symphony Stories."

Throughout our years of travel we were convinced that our school concerts would prove to be one of the constants in a child's development, and we continue of that opinion. So far as we know, the North Carolina Symphony and its Little Symphonies have brought more good music *directly* to the school children over the years than any other orchestra in the nation. That, I hasten to admit, is a claim of substantial proportions. But from the years 1946–71 we have statistics to support our claim:

During that quarter-century span, our Full Symphony and two Little Symphonies played 1,706 free concerts before 3,356,694 school children assembled in audiences that sometimes numbered as many as 6,000. In giving these concerts we traveled 201,909 miles to virtually every corner of the state and occasionally to neighboring states. In those years our performances featured fifty child soloists selected in statewide auditions.

Most importantly perhaps—and surely there is no statistical method of measuring or even estimating such values—our musicians have delighted, thrilled, and inspired by "live" performances and radio broadcasts a host of school children whose lives and leadership continue to enrich the North Carolina way of life.

The Fifties

W E were still deep in the woods with money problems as we entered the decade of the fifties. We sought in every way we could devise to economize, but our economies could go only so far, and each season we were threatened with a large deficit. Nevertheless, membership in the Symphony Society continued to grow through the chapter system, and by 1950 it had reached 20,000.

At Rose Hill in 1950, anticipation of our scheduled appearance was high because of the fact that there had been a successful membership drive to bring the Little Symphony there for the first time. But after seeing the musicians on the stage for the matinee performance at the school, the Symphony chapter chairman and officers realized that the stage was too small for the evening concert. They therefore hurriedly assembled volunteer carpenters and constructed an extension to the stage at the local movie theater, and soon all was in readiness for the evening program. Drafts on the stage at the movie theater were frigid, but the audience was warm, and the coffee served to the musicians backstage was piping hot. We loved the people of Rose Hill and we admired their achievement.

The 1952–53 season was one of our very best. We presented 140 programs in 118 days, traveling many thousands of miles over our hard-circus roads. And we also gave concerts out of the state—in Kingsport, Tennessee; in Gaffney, Greenville, and Georgetown, South Carolina; in Selma, Alabama; and in Welch, West Virginia.

For some of the musicians our long trips, if unrelieved with frequent stops to exercise cramping muscles, were boring and tiring. Others relaxed, settling back in their seats to enjoy naps. Sometimes a group would get together to play cards. Often as we rolled mile after mile we would sing canons and madrigals. Another diversion was exchanging quips about road signs and billboards that we saw in passing.

One road sign near Mount Airy I still recall. It was nailed to the gatepost of the fence enclosing a mountain hut, directly across the road from the welcoming E N T E R sign of an apparently flourishing motel. The little sign at the gate, however, suggested no such hospitality: STAY OUT, it warned, OR GET SHOT OUT! Farther down the road we passed a more reassuring sign. It was a realtor's: WE SELL THE EARTH AND WHAT'S IN IT.

O U R music and our fame continued to spread. In 1952, for example, we made twenty-five radio broadcasts, both within the state and over the national networks of NBC, CBS, and MBS—thus reaching more ears than we could count. And as the radio distributed our sound, journalists were disseminating our story. Such national magazines as *Time, Newsweek, Collier's, Ford Times, Parents' Magazine*—twenty-seven with countrywide circulation—and newspapers of state and regional circulation carried articles pointing out the differences between city orchestras in general and the North Carolina Symphony: the *first* state symphony with no permanent home and no regular rehearsal hall, an orchestra that spent its entire season on the road except for a week of rehearsals preceding the tour of the Little Symphony and another week prior to the full ensemble's tour.

Emphasizing the unique nature of our organization, Howard Taubman at the close of our 1955 tour wrote in the *New York Times*:

> The North Carolina Symphony has now completed ten years as a traveling organization. It has covered 68,000 miles in this decade, playing 664 concerts for grown-ups and children. It has found a touching responsiveness in the audiences.
>
> The orchestra plays standard fare, such as works of Beethoven,

A pleasurable task: helping to tune the children's instruments for participation in the matinee concerts

Brahms, and Mozart, and also does some contemporary pieces. It brings in distinguished soloists, and it gives opportunities to local virtuosos, holding auditions to find young musicians in the area worthy of such appearances.

This is as it should be, and it is a step toward the decentralization of the nation's musical life. Too many young musicians think that no career is possible without the endorsement of a major center like New York. And it has happened in the past that even their own communities paid them no mind until they had won such approval. Even if they have the talent for a larger arena, the experience of playing in their own region could be invaluable.

Mr. Taubman emphasized a salient persuasion of ours, namely, that we should concentrate on discovering outstanding talents around us, and providing opportunities for such talent to develop. That is what "Proff" Koch did at Chapel Hill many decades ago with his Carolina Playmakers.

Another area in which we sought to discover and encourage talent was that of composition. In 1950 we inaugurated our Composers' Auditions, the first winners of which were Robert Darnell of Woman's College, Greensboro, and Margaret Vardell of Salem College; later winners included John Satterfield and Eugene Hemner. These winners received no monetary reward, but they did receive valuable exposure when their compositions were featured in our concerts. In 1953 we were delighted when our generous friend Edward B. Benjamin established the annual Benjamin Award of $1,000 for restful and reposeful music, to be awarded through both the Eastman School of Music at Rochester and the North Carolina Symphony. In Mr. Benjamin's words, the music should be "lovely, soft, slow composition, in either conventional or modern idiom, without vocal or marked percussive effect, and without obtrusive melody." Theron Kirk of Laredo, Texas, was the first recipient of this award in 1954. In 1959 the award became known as the Benjamin Commission.

Among our many lists of the various accomplishments and successes of the North Carolina Symphony over the years, one that brings particular satisfaction is the list of the orchestras with longer seasons and higher salaries to which our players have "graduated." This list includes orchestras in Boston, Philadelphia, Los Angeles, New Orleans, Denver, Indianapolis, San Antonio, Kansas City, New York, Washington, D.C., and Minneapolis. By now, of course, many of our orchestra's members are long gone to other occupations, other enterprises, other states. But I can close my eyes and stand before them on the podium seeing each musician and each instrument as I hear the flow of music.

In keeping with our determination to bring the joy and enrichment of music to all the citizens of the state, we performed public service concerts whenever we were able. In 1954–55 these concerts were attended by children from the state hospital in Morganton, the orthopedic hospital in Asheville, the polio hospital in Greensboro, and the Caswell Training School in Kinston.

Typical of our return engagements was one at Mars Hill College in western North Carolina, where the Little Symphony had played for ten successive years. A makeshift arrangement for our concert there in 1956 was necessary due to the fact that the auditorium at the college had burned, leaving only one large skeletal wall standing. The orchestra was playing a quiet passage in a building across the street when the last wall of the burned-out structure collapsed with a thunderous impact, as the earth shook.

ALTHOUGH the state was generous in raising our fiscal allotment—by 1957 this had reached $30,000 per annum—we still required funds over and above the income from memberships and concert fees. To close the gap we persuaded large corporations and generous individuals to contribute to a fund whose name changed over the years (in the fifties it was first a "Sustaining Fund" and then a "Development Fund") but whose basic purpose was always the same: to keep us solvent. For the fiscal year 1955–56 the difference between our income of $112,895.25 and our expenses was a net profit of $6,858.44; our development fund had reached $8,465.50.

Our income for the season three years later, 1958–59, was some

$5,000 larger—$118,078—but our expenses overran our income: they were $119,000. At that time our Little Symphony fee for the pair of concerts (one adult and one free-admission children's program) was $975, and the fee for the Full Symphony pair was $1,675. We were always most fortunate in that behind our troupe of creative musicians was a busy group of creative fund-raisers. Their work was never-ending, as they helped us spread our musical message. To them I convey my profound thanks.

Legislative Support

N O T A B L E among the long-time supporters of the Symphony have been the North Carolina state legislators, starting with the passage on March 8, 1943, of Senate Bill No. 248, the "horn-tootin'" bill (see above, Chapter 3). A quick look at the legislation enacted during my administration through 1971 will reveal that since the initial appropriation of $4,000 for the biennium 1943–45, placing the North Carolina Symphony under the "patronage and control of the State," the legislators have consistently given their attention to our continuing needs and requirements. State appropriations increased from $4,000 in 1943 to $424,474 for the biennium 1971–73.

But beyond their direct monetary support, the North Carolina legislature assisted us in other valuable ways. An important bill enacted in 1953—G.S. 140-10—enabled us to induce cities and small, rural communities to subscribe for memberships in the North Carolina Symphony Society, thus assisting chapter efforts to bring our orchestra, and our educational programs, to their communities. As an attorney for the state League of Municipalities explained it to us, a municipality may pay for *services provided* but it may not *contribute* to anything. Semantic surgery was therefore performed on the proposed enabling bill, changing the word "contribution" to "payment for services." The bill then passed, and the North Carolina Symphony became eligible to receive tax-free monies to support its programs. Gradually additional subscriptions were obtained from a number of North Carolina cities of varying sizes, including Statesville, Chapel Hill, Durham, Asheville, Raleigh, Hickory, Asheboro, Roanoke Rapids, and others. This legislative action provided another "first" for the North Carolina Symphony.

Other state legislation of importance included authorization of allocations from the state's Contingency and Emergency Fund; permission for United Fund sponsorship and contributions in local communities; the elimination of state privilege license and gross receipts taxes; the provision of retirement privileges for members of the Symphony staff; and the transfer of the North Carolina Symphony to Type II in the State Department of Art, Culture, and History (Type II is more liberal in terms of state control).

We felt, generally, that what we had achieved through legislation had gained because of the confidence the legislators had placed in us and their trust in the integrity of the Symphony and its administration, and we felt that such confidence was justified.

A notable exception was the General Assembly's refusal to go along with our 1959 projected jukebox legislation. In that experience we came to the conclusion that the public interest is not always synonymous with the interest of the public. We had hoped that the legislators would designate as an appropriation to the North Carolina Symphony a portion of the income received from state license taxes on jukeboxes. Such designation would have been in accordance with the policy of some European countries that levy taxes on cabarets and similar enterprises in order to promulgate the arts. The principle was to tax the less desirable activities in favor of providing cultural advantages for the state and the people generally—to let "cheap" music help pay for "good" music.

We estimated that there were at least 9,000 jukebox machines in North Carolina, and our fiscal objective was to tax each machine an additional five dollars. This would have increased our aggregate income by $45,000 a year. The jukebox industry could certainly afford to pay the tax: a year prior to our presenting the proposal, it was reported that the jukebox industry in the United States was grossing approximately $500,000,000 annually.

Unfortunately, our bill, submitted by Representative Watts Hill,

Editorial cartoon by William Sanders of the Greensboro Daily News
(May 24, 1959)

Jr., did not meet with sufficient approval. We were subjected to indiscriminate attacks, including cynical cartoons, editorials, and telephone calls, whose thrust was that we were trying to cause the "ignorant" people to pay for the pleasures of the "rich and arrogant."

I attended one legislative hearing at which an attorney made a presentation in favor of the jukebox operators. He declared to the assembled listeners that he liked "good music," and he admired the North Carolina Symphony. But he added with emphasis that the Symphony should not take a "bite" from the jukebox operators. "It should go where the money is," he suggested in stentorian voice, "and that is to the Appropriations Committee." But that is what we had already done, and the members of that committee had had different ideas.

Ultimately, we were forced to abandon the jukebox proposal. Such opposition notwithstanding, we must all agree that over the years the General Assembly has provided magnanimous support of the Symphony.

O u r relations with the federal government were also preponderantly amicable. From our early days we had paid a federal admissions tax on every membership, without questioning the necessity to do so. But when we were threatened with an increase in this tax, I began to wonder about the legitimacy of its applicability to our situation. Were our memberships really only concert tickets, and thus taxable—or could we justifiably claim that they constituted an educational contribution, and thus save a considerable expenditure?

I consulted friends, including Attorney Richard Thigpen, a tax expert in Charlotte, and Reuben Carlson, a New York lawyer, to ascertain whether anything could be done. But they were unable to suggest any federal tax relief. After trying whatever remedies I thought might help, I determined to proceed directly to the Federal Department of Internal Revenue in Washington.

And that is what I did. But when I arrived there, I was overawed by the task, and I walked several times around the block encompassing the Revenue Building before I could persuade myself to venture into that structure of power to make my request. I did go in, though, and talked for some time with one of the officials. But as we talked, I had the feeling that the situation was hopeless. As I arose to leave, however, the gentleman observed: "Well, if you could show that contributions are *primary* and admissions are *secondary*, it might be possible to consider the matter further."

"That is precisely the point!" I retorted. "I shall write you about it, and promptly." And I did so, and obtained immediate relief from all taxes on memberships on the basis that memberships were primary and admissions to concerts were secondary. Later, our board and the executive committee seemed amazed because we had been plagued so long by this tax problem that had been so quickly resolved. And our new exemption, we realized happily, would save us thousands of dollars each year.

Another tax problem loomed, however: we were threatened by a proposed tax on every mile traveled by each orchestra player in the course of our annual tours. Fortunately, another idea occurred to me, and I proceeded to Raleigh to speak with the gentlemen in the state's Division of Purchases and Contracts, Willis Holding and a Mr. Church.

"Why can't the state rent our buses for us?" I asked them. "Concerts are free to the children. We are performing a public service." The result was that the threatened tax was eliminated altogether, and the state thereafter negotiated the rental of buses for the Symphony's use.

A knotty legal problem arose in connection with our children's concerts. We were determined to bring music to *all* children. In the days of segregation, this meant separate concerts for black and white children in the larger communities. In smaller communities, it meant that black and white children attended the same concert, although they sat in separate sections. Strictly speaking, this was an illegal situation, especially when state-maintained buses were being used to transport the children to the place of the concert. However, when I questioned whether we could somehow make it legal, I was advised *not* to pursue the question further, but to proceed as we had been doing. And as time went on, and our children's programs with their de facto racial desegregation achieved wider acceptance, the problem effectively vanished—even before federal desegregation legislation.

I T became my turn to support the federal government when hearings were held in Washington, D.C., in July 1957 on the subject of establishing a Federal Advisory Commission on the Arts. I was pleased to be invited to testify, for I felt—and still feel—that the benefits from a centralized commission that coordinates and supports the many fine arts activities across the nation have a value beyond measure. After my testimony someone asked me, "Are you not afraid that the government will tell you *what* to play?"

My rather satirical retort was: "We shall be glad to perform the *Blue Danube Waltz* on many occasions if the federal government will honor us with an appropriation!" I learned afterward that the American Symphony League had polled the trustees of many symphony orchestras in the nation and had ascertained that 91 percent of them were against any government subventions. They wished to be independent at that time, but soon they changed their minds and shifted their position when they found it to be to their advantage to do so.

In September 1964 Congress passed a bill called the National Arts and Cultural Development Act, which established a National Arts Council. The council was an advisory board to recommend and encourage the development of cultural resources and to work with local, state, and federal departments on utilization of the arts, both nationally and internationally. It would also explore increased opportunities for the arts. It was thus a step forward, but one which had taken seventy-eight years, for a similar bill had first been introduced in Congress in 1886.

With the passage in September 1965 of an act establishing a National Foundation for the Arts and Humanities, direct grants could be facilitated by organizations and individuals provided certain conditions were met. That same September the National Arts and Humanities Act was passed by both houses of Congress. The bill defined the arts as music, painting, architecture, drama, dance, creative writing, sculpture, industrial design, folk art, graphic and craft arts, motion pictures, radio, television, et al. In other words, the arts related to presentation, exhibition, and performance. The bill provided for workshops to develop appreciation of the arts by the citizenry, and it also embraced research, surveys, and planning for the arts. Truly, our legislators have worked well to support our efforts to bring to the people a developing interest in the arts.

Road Notes

T H E life of an orchestra on wheels is seldom dull. Fortunately, however, the shared vicissitudes of touring—the frustrations and felicities—have the ability to generate a cohesiveness of experience and goals that generally outweighs the instances of disunity.

On our tours about the state, we Symphony members were said to live out of our suitcases—an apt description. Our suitcase "homes" depended upon our obtaining hotel or motel reservations with adequate rooms for all members of the orchestra. Such a hostelry would be the center from which we would fan out to perform concerts in outlying communities.

Returning year after year to hotels that were allowed to deteriorate, we became inured to windows nailed down with layers of dust on their panes, skimpy draperies or Venetian blinds that would not close, a stark light so high over the bed that one could barely turn it off without standing on the bed or climbing a ladder, drawers that stuck in shabby furniture, only one rickety luggage rack in a narrow room listed as a double, mattresses soft and lumpy, faucets that dripped all night, and radiators that hissed and banged. Maxine soon learned to keep a supply of extension cords and light bulbs in her suitcase in order to have a proper reading light. Happily, most of these hotels—"homey monsters," as one of the musicians labeled them—by this time have been demolished.

The proprietors of one such place were a worthy Belgian couple who had found a new life for themselves in America and were making valiant efforts to serve the public in an old building sadly in need of renovation and repairs. While we were waiting one day for lunch to be served, several musicians were on the balcony and one was speaking disparagingly of the outmoded furniture's condition. He said he was afraid to venture sitting down. Albin Pikutis was quick to respond.

"Aw, that sofa's old and battered a little," Albin said, "but it's OK."

To prove it, Albin sat down on the sofa—and crashed with it to the floor.

As the personnel manager of the orchestra was checking in the musicians at another of these hotels, he noticed a sign displayed at the registration counter: "You don't have to be dumb to be a hotel manager, but it helps." He offered no comment, but inwardly agreed; and the general appearance of the hostelry supported the sign. But the delicious buttermilk, corn bread, and "home cooking" in some of the old hotels, such as in Forest City, Lumberton, Salisbury, and Mount Airy, compensated for declining accommodations.

Living in these hostelries and in such proximity to one another during almost continuous travel in the winter months, the Little Symphony musicians sometimes showed increasing irritation. For reasons of economy, and also because hotels and motels infrequently had enough single rooms, our musicians generally were assigned to double rooms. Privacy became a rare privilege. Nerves were frayed. You might hear one woman describing her roommate: "She has a voice that would cut glass," or "Her voice sounds like three pennies in a milk bottle." And one cold, foggy morning in the mountains, as we were boarding the bus, we heard a bride mumbling to her husband, paraphrasing Falstaff, "What an awful way to *yearn* a living!"

In the days before the coming of new motels, the old hostelries in small towns were often places where people met for banquets and wedding suppers and parties, and particularly for Sunday family dinners. One such meeting place was the old Blue Ridge Hotel in Mt. Airy (a thriving town some forty-two miles northwest of Winston-Salem, many of whose residents pronounce the name "Mount

Awry"). The most notable feature of the Blue Ridge, aside from its delicious cuisine, was Claude, who ran the elevator, carried suitcases, waited on tables, and served as general factotum. He had good reason to feel possessive about the hotel, for he had worked there for many years and his sovereignty was unchallenged. Once, after a disagreement with the management, Claude fired himself and obtained a job at the local post office. But when he discovered a few days later that his old job had been filled by someone else, he returned to the hotel, fired the new incumbent, and proceeded forthwith to insert himself into the vacancy. He reasoned he had a stake in the old hotel, and he certainly understood the law of possession.

Maxine and I were generally assigned the same room, year after year, on the second floor overlooking the town's main street. The window of the bathroom went down to the floor, and the commode was directly in front of the window and close to the outside air. On the tank of the toilet was a cigar box containing loose pieces of toilet tissue. Although there was a Venetian blind at the bathroom window, it could not always be cajoled into closing. The rugs in our bedroom were dusty, and sometimes large holes in them were covered by overstuffed furniture. And one had to be careful of the stair landings in the dimly lighted balcony. Usually we were in Mt. Airy during the income-tax return preparation period, and the only place where we could spread out our pages of tax materials and forms was in the balcony area.

One year, the Symphony's presence in Mt. Airy made even more of an impact than usual. We had a soloist, a European tenor with a powerful voice. He could find no place to vocalize in the old Blue Ridge Hotel with its thin walls, and so he went for a walk in search of a deserted area where he could practice. After much walking, he came upon a cemetery where he thought he might practice unobserved and unheard.

But it didn't work out that way. Through her kitchen window that opened toward the cemetery, a housewife heard unusual sounds as the soloist warmed to his practicing, and peering through the window she saw a strange man lustily serenading an impassive and unresponding audience of cold tombstones.

Quickly she went to the telephone and called the police, who raced to the cemetery. They were incredulous when the stranger told them he was to be soloist that evening with the North Carolina Symphony Orchestra, but his strong, high-pitched tenor voice convinced them. With much deference the police proceeded to drive their talented guest back to the hotel where they left him with us after a round of handshakes and friendly good-byes.

When the orchestra played in Lumberton in the early 1950s, we were lodged in the old Lumberton Hotel, distinguished for its brand of Southern hospitality and its Sunday dinners. But I don't remember the Sunday dinners there as vividly as I do watching the moviegoers arriving at the theater across the street and entering it through three separate doorways: one marked W H I T E S, another N E G R O E S, and the third, I N D I A N S. Happily, the times—at least in that respect—have since changed for the better.

I A M sure that none of the orchestra's veterans seriously yearns for the return of those good old days of quaint overnight lodging. But there *were* experiences during those years of traveling that I would delight in reliving—such as, for example, when we musicians were guests for tea in the charming Warrenton home of gracious Katherine Arrington, a faithful and effective long-time supporter of the arts.

Warrenton, in eastern Carolina, like Warrenton, Virginia, is an old community with an illustrious heritage. As Maxine and I arrived at the small Hotel Warrenton with members of our Little Symphony, snow was beginning to fall, and it continued falling until the village was blanketed and we were indeed snowbound. We had other concerts scheduled for that section of the state over the next several days, but nothing was left for us but to call ahead and postpone our engagements. We were in Warrenton ten snowbound days, and despite the weather, it was a delightful stay we had there. The local citizens welcomed the Little Symphony with a warmth of

Musicians "at home" on the bus
(Reprinted from The Lamp *[Standard Oil Company newsletter], March*
1953; courtesy The Lamp, *Exxon Corporation)*

hospitality that resembled football homecomings. Our musicians were caught up in a whirlwind of entertainments. How beautiful were the unscheduled musicales when the Warrentonians opened their homes during our "white vacation"!

On Sunday morning Maxine and I attended church and there Mrs. Arrington invited us to bring the musicians to her home that afternoon for tea. We thanked her and assured her we would bring as many as were free to come. We were somewhat uneasy about the sort of response her invitation would get from the musicians, so we asked the personnel manager to extend the invitation. When he knocked on hotel room doors, he interrupted siestas, shampooing, letter-writing, clothes-washing, and preparation of oboe reeds. Nevertheless, about fifteen of us bundled up, braved the snow, and deposited our galoshes at Mrs. Arrington's door promptly at four o'clock that afternoon, and we enjoyed the welcome and the warmth and elegance of her beautiful home.

Upon being seated at the long mahogany table in the dining room, with its long-stemmed goblets, cut-glass finger bowls, and glass plates sparkling in the candlelight, and with its gossamer doilies on the plates beneath the finger bowls, we experienced a small shiver of apprehension. Would an innocently done faux pas betray us? When a large dish of ice cream was served to Maxine, she made a deliberate display of removing the delicate doily *with* the finger bowl; but our hostess saved the day by remarking in a firm voice, "Do you know, one time I turned to one of my guests and noticed he was chewing one of my doilies!"

As it had done so memorably at Warrenton, the weather sometimes played a strong hand in the orchestra's being unable to fulfill immediate concert commitments. Once a cameraman from the National Broadcasting Company arrived to cover a children's concert in Rocky Mount where we were scheduled to play in a ball park. This time snow was not the problem: it rained, it poured! The performance had to be canceled, and we missed the opportunity of a nationwide broadcast.

Another time the weather defeated us when a storm prevented our crossing Pamlico Sound to Ocracoke where we were scheduled to play for an audience assembled on the Outer Banks. We had played at Campbell College at Buies Creek the night before, but a savage snowstorm struck as we were heading eastward and the weather turned bitterly cold. Crossing the Sound from the mainland to Ocracoke Island would be perilous, it was agreed, and the authorities refused to sanction such a venture. And had we been able to make the crossing, the only accommodations available to us on the island would have been in a small hotel without any heating.

A *Life Magazine* photographer was awaiting us in the old Hotel Jefferson at Morehead City when the orchestra checked in that Friday night. While the snow and sleet held us confined, the photographer stayed with us until late Sunday afternoon before abandoning his plans to photograph the Little Symphony performing at Ocracoke Island. Two days later the weather cleared, but the *Life* correspondent had been reassigned to cover a story in Washington, D.C.

We were disappointed, of course. We wouldn't see ourselves in a *Life Magazine* layout. But more disappointing was our realization that canceling the Ocracoke engagement meant that there would be no emulation of our earlier reception at Cape Hatteras, where we had been honored with a Saturday night square dance and a Sunday morning drive along the dunes with the Coast Guard.

That day's experience had been memorable. The guardsmen had pointed out old wrecks from World War II, and the fisherfolk islanders had regaled us with lively accounts of German spies operating in that region, and of other grotesque happenings. We were told, for example, that there had been a strange "lady" who had stayed for a time in Southport. She was well dressed and seemed courteous and cultivated.

But she always wore gloves.

She attended local social functions and mingled easily with the people in the community. During the daytime she would take her palette and paint box to the shore to paint seascapes, with her gloves on. After a while she departed and went north, perhaps to New Jersey. Later, word came back to North Carolina that the "lady" had been discovered to be a man, a German spy who was apprehended by the American authorities. The gloves the lady had worn so faithfully had concealed, we were told, easily identifiable masculine hands. What finally became of her (or him), we would never know. But it was an intriguing story, one of the strangest of the many related to us in our travels throughout colorful North Carolina.

O N one tour we were lodged at the Hickory Hotel, from which we were to travel to concerts in Catawba County communities. After a matinee performance at one of the county schools our stage manager had the foresight to stop our bus in nearby Newton long enough to set up our equipment for the night's program in the high school auditorium. We then went on to the Hickory Hotel for our evening meal.

We were returning to Newton along the twelve-mile stretch of highway when a downpour burst upon us to delay our arrival, and when our bus did draw up in the school's parking area, the building was dark and the doors were locked. Some of the musicians managed to pry open a basement window and get into the auditorium, where they recovered the tympani and music racks from the dark stage and reloaded them on our bus. Then we set off to search for *another* high school and the restive audience that would be awaiting our arrival.

Thirty minutes later we came upon a large building with lights blazing and a mass of cars parked about it. Quickly we piled out, waded through puddles, and, tracking red mud through a side door, walked onto the stage to the generous applause of the patient audience. We were surprised and relieved at the warmth of the reception accorded us. Later, we were told that the chapter chairman had admitted to the audience that he had forgotten to inform the Symphony office of the change in the concert's location.

On another occasion we knew where we were supposed to go for an evening concert, but we lost our way and were again late in arriving. Our suitcase-home on that tour was in West Jefferson, where cuisine and room accommodations were ample for housing the orchestra while we gave concerts within a radius of forty miles. We had an experienced bus driver named McAllister—everybody called him "Mac"—who was skilled not only in handling a bus in all kinds of weather and traffic situations but also in setting up a well-timed travel schedule anticipating detours and traffic delays.

We were scheduled to give a concert that evening in Sparta, some thirty miles northeastward. We left West Jefferson with ample time to spare, but Mac took a wrong turn into a sharply ascending mountain road that led us into a cul-de-sac, a high school parking area. A basketball game was in progress and the closely parked cars prevented a turn of the bus in any direction. Nor could Mac extricate us by putting the bus in reverse. We did the only thing we could do, which was to go inside the gymnasium and ask that the game be interrupted long enough for several of the car owners to move their cars and provide sufficient turning-around space for the bus to maneuver its way out.

At Sparta we found a forgiving, friendly audience, composed in large part of people who had been hosts and supporters of the orchestra's concerts in that community during many past seasons. These people understood that mountain driving in the nighttime might well cause a delay in the beginning of a concert.

The start of yet another concert was delayed when our music librarian left the entire cabinet of orchestra folders backstage in Greensboro and he didn't discover his oversight until we were arriving for our concert in Lexington. He hopped on the Symphony bus and in subdued tones confessed to me what he had done.

Soon the audience would be arriving—but with no music there could be no concert, and between Lexington and Greensboro were some thirty miles of curving, twisting two-lane highway. Our poor librarian telephoned Greensboro to ask that the auditorium be unlocked so the music might be recovered, and a car was sent racing to get it. As the hour arrived for the concert to begin, the announcer told the assembled audience what had happened. The concert would begin with the arrival of the music, he promised. And it would not be cut short, nor would the audience be unduly late in getting home.

"What we are going to do tonight, you see," he went on to explain, "is something different. This evening we are going to have the intermission *before* the concert begins!"

That's just what we did. The audience stirred about the auditorium or sat patiently as the "intermission" proceeded. When the music arrived, after not too long a delay, the concert began. The audience applauded us heartily, and the next day's newspapers gave us generous reviews.

A DIFFERENT sort of problem with which we were occasionally forced to contend was *dogs*. I remember a concert on a warm spring evening in Chapel Hill, when a dog sauntered down the wide center aisle of Memorial Hall as an oboe solo was being played in the overture to *The Gypsy Baron*, by Johann Strauss, Jr. Calmly the dog proceeded the length of the aisle and ascended the steps leading to the center of the stage. There he stood transfixed, silhouetted against the bright lights, listening to the oboe solo. Then, after sniffing the conductor, he turned and deliberately retraced his way down the steps and along the aisle to the exit, still little impressed by the audience or the music.

I shall always wonder what prompted that dog to sample our concert. Recalling that evening brings immediately to mind another Symphony concert in which a dog had a leading role.

We played a children's concert in Asheville at which the movement of Ferde Grofé's *Hudson River Suite* entitled "Rip Van Winkle" intrigued some of the adults in attendance, and they requested it as an encore during that evening's concert. During the playing of this selection, following the specifications in the score, we utilized a tape-recorded dog bark, which was cued in several times in a raucous rhythm, apparently dog language.

That night as we were playing the encore and came to the first barking, three loud answering barks came from the rear of the auditorium. The audience was startled, and so, of course, were the musicians, who had no idea where the sound was coming from. When we came to the next taped barking, there was no answering bark, only silence. As we left the auditorium, we were still wondering about the ebullient interruption. How had it happened?

Several months later Maxine and I were in an elevator in the towering Asheville City Hall when the elevator stopped and a blind girl with a large German police dog entered. Maxine introduced herself to the girl, whom she recognized as one of the members of our Asheville Symphony chapter. In the course of the conversation Maxine suddenly recalled the episode of the impromptu dog barks.

"Did you attend our Symphony concert last spring?" she asked the blind girl.

"Yes, I did," the girl told her.

"Did you hear the selection 'Rip Van Winkle' with the dog barks?"

"Yes, I did."

"Tell me, was that your dog that answered the recorded barks with such energy?"

"Yes, it was."

"But the dog *stopped* barking," Maxine pursued the puzzle. "How did you stop him?"

"I *told* him to stop," the young lady said.

This was the first time that we realized that a dog has its own tone-line, pitch, and rhythm, just as an individual has his own language. Especially notable had been the identical rhythm and pitch. It had been truly a dog's dialogue, and the dog on our tape was evidently another German police dog (the breed was *not* specified in the score!).

There was a sign in front of the Undergraduate Library at the University of North Carolina at Chapel Hill some years ago: D E A R D O G , P L E A S E S T A Y O U T . The sign further invited canine attention by including a drawing of a dog, and by being attached at dog-eye level to the lower portion of the door. But when the weather was cold and rainy I was forced to the conclusion that even some Chapel Hill dogs must be illiterate or ill-mannered, because they walked right past the sign to congregate at a warm spot *inside*.

I N addition to the general adversities that were shared by all the personnel of the orchestra, there were some that were inflicted upon the Swalins in particular. Such a one occurred in our early years, when the orchestra was scheduled for a performance in Elizabeth City. Maxine's teaching duties had prevented her from accompanying the orchestra to Elizabeth City for the afternoon rehearsal, but she had been careful to instruct her maid in the packing of my suitcase with full-dress clothes and accessories, and had emphasized the fact that I would need *everything* on the packing list for the performance.

Her teaching day finished, Maxine took the bus for Elizabeth City and arrived backstage a few minutes before eight o'clock. In the ladies' dressing room she found everyone in a tizzy of hardly restrained amusement.

"What's going on?" the puzzled Maxine asked. "What in the world—"

"Just wait until you see your husband!" One of the ladies pointed toward the men's dressing room door. "He'll be coming out in a minute. They're in there fixing him up!"

About that time I emerged.

I was indeed a vision of sartorial splendor: full-dress perfection—tails, pleated shirt, white tie, pearl studs and cuff links, black shoes and socks—and pistol-legged dark blue serge trousers borrowed from the tall, thin husband of one of the musicians and precariously held together at the belt-line by safety pins, because the zipper had refused to zip. Over this all-too-apparent makeshift arrangement, my eagerly helpful fellow-musicians had draped a vast cummerbund hastily commandeered from the orchestra's rotund tympanist.

This Elizabeth City performance was given during the World War II era, a time when the nation was alive with patriotic fervor that was demonstrated in the spirited playing of the national anthem before every concert.

How well I remember that evening as I stood up to face the audience, how disturbingly real the sudden feeling of panic that engulfed me. Should I, could I, risk acknowledging the audience's cordial welcome with a deep bow? I smiled grimly, closed my eyes, bowed low from the waist, and listened intently.

The accelerating applause was thunderously polite. I heard not a snicker, nor a guffaw, nor the faintest sound of a garment ripping. I opened my eyes. The cummerbund had not slipped down to hobble my ankles. The safety pins had held. And I raised my arms to signal the *Star-Spangled Banner*.

DRESSING for concert appearances caused trouble more than once. At Asheboro, in an old elementary school that no longer exists, Maxine and I changed clothes in a room adjoining the stage. When we tried to enter the stage the doorknob came off, and when we pounded on the door we could make no one hear because the hornists were warming up their instruments. We were contemplating exiting through a window to the ground by using a long Mexican shawl, when we finally secured the attention of someone on the stage. But it required screwdrivers before the stage manager and several assistants could open the door.

Near Winston-Salem, the orchestra was to present a concert in a new auditorium that had just been completed. But the only private dressing room was down spiral stairs to a small, ill-lighted, dank room without heat, chairs, or hooks in the wall. We looked for another room where I might change clothes after the concert and before the reception that was to be held in the same building, and the only possibility was a little closet in the front of the stage, where a rose arbor had been stored. In dressing there, I discovered that even *artificial* roses can have thorns!

T H E thorns in our hard-circus road seemed to outnumber the roses from time to time, but never for very long. More often, our mishaps along the way, of which this chapter provides but a small sampling, furnished a lively counterpoint to our serious work of bringing music to the people. For those of us who believed in our mission, ours was a joyous journey.

The Sixties

THE period from 1960 to 1972 (the year of my last concert) was a time of major changes and challenges for the Symphony. The grandest of these, in my opinion, was the Ford Foundation Challenge Campaign, which I have allotted a chapter of its own (Chapter 14).

In 1960, because of unprecedented heavy snowstorms in April, our fifteenth annual tour was not completed until *June*. While we were snowed in at Hendersonville, near Asheville, we fell seventeen concerts behind schedule. Bills mounted at the Skyland Hotel, while our income diminished to nothing. Orchestra members grew bored, and no one seemed disposed to rehearse, because it appeared to be without purpose. That experience revealed clearly that a musician has little incentive without an audience.

When friends and supporters of our orchestra learned that the unusually severe weather conditions were keeping us from fulfilling the concert commitments that would have financed our touring, they hastened to our rescue. Johnsie Burnham of Chapel Hill and other friends started an emergency fund of $416 that soon was augmented to $780.

This "emergency" increased our awareness that among the orchestra's other financial needs was an ongoing, permanent fund—an endowment, in other words. Such a fund would generate interest to facilitate our hoped-for expansion, and it would provide an asset against which money could be borrowed should a real emergency arise.

We were encouraged to embark on our campaign for an endowment by two surprising gifts. Imagine our delight when at Christmas 1960 we received a holiday greeting from Mrs. Eli T. Watson, of New York and Hickory, with a check for $5,000! And in 1961 a thriller indeed: an independent bequest from the estate of Elsie F. Holder of East Orange, New Jersey, to the amount of $34,657.41. We had not known Mrs. Holder, but evidently she had read an article in the *Ford Times* on the North Carolina Symphony Orchestra, and she had written to us requesting information about our tax status and our programs. After complying with her request, we were notified that the Symphony had been included in her will.

But even with such magnanimous gifts to the orchestra, we would require a strong campaign in order to establish and nourish an endowment. For some time we had entertained the idea of an annual Symphony Ball to raise money for the Symphony's expansion. Maxine, however, was less than enthusiastic; for she was apprehensive that in time such a ball might become a political and social expedient, and detract from the concept of the Symphony as a people's orchestra. Nevertheless, our Society officers generally agreed that it might be a profitable venture, and we set out to interest organizations or individuals in sponsoring a ball.

As initial sponsors, we first approached the Junior League of Raleigh. Maxine and I had recorded for the Junior League a set of twelve programs for broadcast by WPTF, Raleigh, for the city schools. But when we approached them on the subject of the ball, they were unable to assist. In true Symphony tradition, however, this defeat was only a temporary setback. And another first for North Carolina was achieved when Johnsie Burnham, Mrs. Charles E. Johnson, Mrs. Harmon Duncan (later Mrs. Dan Edwards), and Ed Rankin succeeded in 1961, with the strong support of Governor and Mrs. Terry Sanford, in organizing the first North Carolina Symphony Ball, which was given at the Governor's Mansion. It was a thoroughly delightful occasion, and it provided a net profit of $11,049.30 for our Endowment Fund.

Eleanor Steber, soloist at the Symphony Ball
(Durham Morning Herald *photo by Harold Moore)*

Two years later, at the 1963 Symphony Ball in the Mansion, our soloist, Eleanor Steber of the Metropolitan Opera, was singing when a racial demonstration erupted outside. Several hundred people, many of them carrying flaming torches, were screaming demands for a confrontation with Governor Terry Sanford. To appease them, Governor Sanford stepped out on the veranda and offered to meet with representatives of the crowd at his office on the following Monday. They had called for immediate action, but cooler heads prevailed, his proposal was accepted, and the crowd dispersed.

Interestingly, thirteen years later, in March 1976, we received a call from the State Department of Cultural Resources inquiring whether we had taped the music that night while the racial demonstration was occurring outside. The official who was telephoning explained that he was in search of background music for a film being prepared for the National Bicentennial observance entitled "The Right of Dissent." But we could not help him. The concert and the demonstration, unfortunately, had not been recorded.

After 1964 the Symphony Balls were held in locations other than the Governor's Mansion in Raleigh—in such places, for example, as the Morehead Planetarium in Chapel Hill, Minges Coliseum at East Carolina University in Greenville, and the North Carolina Country Club in Pinehurst. Because North Carolina covers such a wide area from east to west, two Symphony Balls were held in 1970: the Azalea Ball in Wilmington and, one week later, the Western Ball at the Grove Park Inn in Asheville. The most successful financially was the ball for the 1968–69 season, which netted a profit of $15,209.58.

Judge and Mrs. L. Richardson Preyer of Greensboro served in 1961 as first Symphony Ball chairmen. They and their successors (see Appendix I) made certain that "beauty *is* a Symphony Ball" and that flowers and music enhanced the magic of the gala occasions. These balls brought great pleasure to the participants while they furnished needed funds for the Symphony Society treasury. Initially, as I have said, they fed our Endowment Fund, which by 1966 had reached $50,942.02. Then, starting in 1967, when our Ford Chal-

Governor and Mrs. Moore enjoying the Symphony Ball
(Reprinted from The Raleigh Times *by permission of The News and Observer*
Publishing Co., Raleigh, North Carolina; courtesy of the North Carolina
Department of Archives and History)

lenge Campaign was under way, the proceeds from the balls helped make up the annual Maintenance Fund that was one of the stipulations of the Ford grant challenge.

Meanwhile, contributions continued to come into the orchestra's coffers. By our eighteenth annual tour in 1963, there were also appropriations from cities and counties that allocated funds to local campaigns of Symphony Society chapters. Municipal authorities, as well as parents and teachers, were becoming convinced that bringing the North Carolina Symphony to their communities was a worthwhile achievement. We began to witness a coming of age in musical taste. The first, second, and third decades of listeners were becoming confident that there was fine metal in orchestral music. It was a heritage—a promise—and our reward came in the responses of the children wherever the sound carried. Having heard Mozart, Haydn, Bach, and later classics in the elementary grades, they were beginning to attend evening concerts as teenagers. Children's audiences in the 1963 season, our records disclose, totaled 149,917.

A PROBLEM that had plagued us since our early days persisted into the sixties: the lack of a permanent rehearsal hall. One season we rehearsed in an old school recreation hall, which we had to vacate after school hours because of basketball practice. The heating facilities included a noisy blower system; the musicians seated near the blowers felt themselves being slowly baked, while those more remote were shivering. But to the basketball players chasing up and down the floor the situation was not uncomfortable, and who would have had the temerity to suggest that basketball practice might not be more important than horn-tootin' rehearsals?

At Chapel Hill, because of my relationship with the University as a former member of the faculty, the University generously provided rent-free office space to the Symphony—first in Swain Hall, next in a barracks, and then in trailers—but we had an ongoing hope that we might secure a permanent Symphony home in Chapel Hill with rehearsal headquarters. It was in 1967 that I asked Chancellor Carlyle Sitterson to petition the University for an enlargement of Memorial Hall, with the result that he sought a legislative appropriation of $900,000 to provide an addition of 12,000 square feet to that auditorium. The request, however, was voted down by the Advisory Budget Commission.

Other cities "wooed" us from time to time, in a way reminiscent of the earlier efforts of other North Carolina communities to be named as sites for projected colleges, such as those in Laurinburg and Rocky Mount. Their interest tended to wane, however, when they became acquainted with the extent of our needs.

Raleigh mounted an intensive campaign in 1967, with the result that throughout the 1967–68 season the orchestra rehearsed in that city. Our offices were still in Chapel Hill, however. And the following season rehearsals were moved to the Erwin Auditorium Arts and Crafts Center in Durham, where they remained—thanks to the generosity of the Durham Recreation Department—for several years.

It was not until 1975 that a single, "permanent" home was found with adequate office and rehearsal space: in Raleigh's extensively custom-renovated Memorial Auditorium. Attracting the North Carolina Symphony was one of the facets of Raleigh's urban revitalization plan, and the city exerted itself to meet the needs of the musicians in every way possible.

A MAJOR change in our operations took place in 1967, when we extended our season by two months and added a second Little Symphony. For the first time, all our personnel were engaged for the orchestra's full season. The Full Symphony toured from November through February; it then divided into two Little Symphonies, which toured independently, one in the eastern part of the state and one in the west, during March and April.

To celebrate our new identity, Maxine consulted with the Blue Bell Foundation on the design of a new evening dress for the ladies of the orchestra. The result was a pattern in various sizes that allowed for vigorous playing activities during evening concerts. The dress had a smooth, uncluttered neckline, softly folded side pleats, and contoured full-length sleeves. Patterns were mailed to the musicians, who sewed their own black dresses prior to the 1967–68 season.

The following year the Morganton Dyeing and Finishing Corporation generously provided material for new skirts to be worn at matinee performances. And yet another ladies' costume change occurred in 1970, when the latest fashion of mini-skirts threatened the dignity of the orchestra's presentations. The new matinee and travel apparel suggested by the designers at the Blue Bell Foundation, and provided to us at cost, was a pantsuit ensemble in blue wool with a white striped blouse and jumper.

A most happy innovation in this period, and one that I hoped would become an annual occurrence, was inaugurated in the 1968–69 season when we collaborated with the North Carolina School of the Arts to present Tchaikovsky's *Nutcracker Ballet*—not just the suite, but the actual ballet! The performances were so well received that we featured excerpts from the ballet at the Symphony Ball the following spring.

One of my dreams for the day when the Symphony would have a permanent home and a nearly year-round schedule was that it would also have a resident ballet troupe and, eventually, at least a part-time opera company—thus expanding the avenues through which the richness of music might reach our audiences.

CONTRIBUTIONS and assistance continued to come our way. The number of applicants in our Young Adult Auditions was increasing, and there was an urgency for a special budget to cover the mounting costs of renting scores and parts for concerto literature and the rental of pianos, as well as to increase the honoraria for judges and award-winning soloists. In 1970 we were assisted financially by Mrs. D. McLauchlin Faircloth, who provided an initial gift of $25,000 in honor of her parents. The auditions thenceforth became the "Kathleen and Joseph M. Bryan Auditions."

In 1970 we were further honored by a grant of $25,000 from the National Endowment for the Arts. The money was to be applied specifically to our operating expenses; its purpose, as stated by the Endowment, was "to lengthen the 1970–71 season in order to make possible longer employment of orchestra staff and to broaden the cultural opportunities of young people in the area served by the Symphony."

That grant served us well: the 1970–71 season was extended by two weeks, and we employed five additional musicians. We also finished that season with an unprecedented estimated cash surplus of $16,000!

CHAPTER 12

The Music

SERGE KOUSSEVITZKY once said that "You must bring your music to the masses and the masses will come to you." This is what we have tried to do by taking the North Carolina Symphony *to the people*. Our mission, unlike that of a city symphony, has been predominantly educational and cultural in reaching citizens and young people of rural as well as urban centers. The "masses" were, above all, the children.

Through the years our programs were based upon what we regarded as good music. It was the kind of music we hoped our listeners would *experience*, for we believed that the Symphony must lead the way, as educators seek to guide the course of learning in colleges and universities. We were hoping and trying thus to chart the direction of the public taste in accordance with the principle enunciated by a psychologist who held that "one learns exactly the reactions that he practices."

But what *is* good music? How does one tell what constitutes good taste in music or in the allied arts, or what will be permanent? And what is the *artistic purpose* of a work of art? Justice Cardozo once referred to his method of reaching a decision in a difficult legal case: "I think about it; I think about it; I think about it; and then I get a feeling"—and so it can be in music in the pursuit of excellence.

One should really speak of "musics," for there are so many different kinds of music. We endeavored to cover a broad spectrum of national origins, periods, and styles in our program selections. We

Illustrating an expressive passage

tried also to encourage superior choices in choral music, and we anticipated that high school students in particular would study excerpts from the choral masterpieces. For that purpose we assigned to outstanding high school choruses specific selections for study toward performances with the North Carolina Symphony.

The essence of any sensuous art is the evocation of feeling and understanding. A combination of the arts can be effective in creating emotional reactions. For example, I shall not soon forget our Christmas performance of Tchaikovsky's *Nutcracker Ballet* with a fine cast from the North Carolina School of the Arts. It was a moving experience, with performing dancers ranging in age from perhaps twelve to twenty or older. The settings of the ballet were sumptuous, the dancing and acting superb, and the score of the ballet was inspiring.

We found that of all the styles, Romantic music was by far the most acceptable to adult audiences, especially the works of Beethoven, Brahms, Chopin, Liszt, Schubert, Schumann, and Wagner.

Opinion polls also revealed that French and American composers were of secondary interest, in spite of our efforts to promote them. Even Gershwin, with his *Rhapsody in Blue*, failed to win significant popularity. A study of record catalogues indicates that Bach and Handel rank high, especially with the progress of music education in American colleges and universities, and we found, indeed, that when we performed the works of these and other Baroque composers they were well received by our audiences.

Our desire to provide a broad range of music was hindered at times by our resources. The large works of the late Romantics, such as Mahler and Bruckner, would have necessitated the hiring of additional personnel, an option that was not generally open to us due to fiscal or logistical limitations. Furthermore, the music rental fees for large works, as well as for contemporary music, can be excessive.

T H E presentation of contemporary music was an area in which we were not always successful—but the North Carolina Symphony was not unique in this regard. I once overheard an intelligent-looking gentleman declare to his companion, as he left a Philharmonic concert in Carnegie Hall at the intermission: "This is a lot of garbage!" The composition they had just heard was a concert version of a modern opera by Milhaud. The lights in the hall were too dim to enable the audience to read the program notes, however; the two men had attended the concert for enjoyment, but they went away with nothing. At least our sports programs do better than that, because there are commentators who explain the progress of the action of football, basketball, or hockey games.

In North Carolina, there were occasions when the music seemed so difficult to comprehend that we tried to prepare our audience in advance with pertinent oral program notes delivered by a commentator from the stage. Some of the selections for which we used this technique were Stravinsky's *L'Histoire du Soldat* (The Soldier's Story), Ives's *Unanswered Question*, Schoenberg's *Pieces for Orchestra*, Hovhaness's *Mysterious Mountain*, and Rorem's *Lions*. Although speech is not a substitute for music, the right words can shed some light upon enjoyment and learning.

In addition to preparing the audience in advance of a concert when the music seems enigmatical, it is sometimes essential to prepare the musicians as well. My listing of Rorem's *Lions* brings to mind the concert when we had as guest performer an adroit jazz pianist from Charlotte named Loonis McGlohon. As Mr. McGlohon later described the experience to a friend,

> One of the biggest surprises of my life came the night when Dr. Swalin called me on the telephone to ask if I would be a guest performer with the North Carolina Symphony. He explained that we would be doing a contemporary work by Ned Rorem, a piece called *Lions*.
>
> Thinking that Dr. Swalin had me confused with some concert pianist, I reminded him quickly that I was a jazz pianist, and that playing under him with that fine orchestra would scare me to death, because I would be out of my class. But he assured me that the piece was jazz-oriented, and he added, "It's a piece about lions; so you will be able to roar."
>
> I was really nervous at the first rehearsal, especially when the double bassist of my trio came out on the stage barefooted. For a jazz musician, facing a battery of string players is hard enough, but in this case I was much more intimidated by the maestro's tall and elegant bearing. But suddenly he seemed less formidable when he said to the orchestra and to my trio players, "In this piece, he will go along on *his* way, and we shall do much the same. With good luck, we shall end together."
>
> It was good to learn that Dr. Swalin was interested in American jazz. It helped to humanize him for me. I thank him for doing away with the fear I had always had of symphony orchestra conductors.

I appreciate Loonis McGlohon's comments, though it had never occurred to me that I needed to be humanized. And I *do* like American jazz.

Two sisters of the Trapp family in costume for a children's concert
(Courtesy of the UNC Photo Lab)

I N spite of our best efforts, there were always listeners whose choice of music differed. Once Maxine was on an elevator returning to her room in a Burlington hotel after one of our concerts, when she overheard this bit of conversation between two gentlemen:

"Here we travel all the way from Brooklyn to *this* place and have to listen to Britten's *Sea Interludes*! At home we could have heard some Tchaikovsky or Rachmaninoff! What is this orchestra trying to do, anyway?"

What the Symphony was trying to do was to present programs that would give the audiences and the musicians aesthetic fulfillment. And I believe that, on the whole, we were successful.

As an example, for the 1957 season the Full Symphony prepared a Bach chorale prelude, Brahms's *Symphony No. 1*, Beethoven's *Symphony No. 4*, Strauss's tone poem *Don Juan*, Vaughan-Williams's *Fantasia on a Theme by Thomas Tallis*, and Tchaikovsky's overture-fantasy *Romeo and Juliet*; and the Little Symphony prepared Liszt's *Hungarian Rhapsody No. 14*, an overture by Handel, Mozart's *Symphony No. 38* ("Prague"), and Larsson's *Pastoral Suite*, as well as other short works.

That same season the children heard works by Purcell, Bach, Debussy, Wagner, and Prokofiev; and spaced among this music, they lustily sang songs they had learned for the program, such as "This Land Is Your Land," or a chorale from Bach's *Christmas Oratorio*.

During that 1957 season the evening audiences heard two previous audition soloists who had become favorites with audiences and therefore were presented during several seasons: they were Fred Sahlmann, a pianist who had studied in Vienna on a Fulbright fellowship before returning to teach at Elon College, his alma mater; and Walter Carringer, a tenor from Murphy, who joined the faculty at Northwestern University after transcontinental tours as soloist with the Robert Shaw Chorale. The adult audition winners in 1957 were Edwin Blanchard, baritone, and Nicholas Zumbro, pianist.

T H E symphonic literature performed by our orchestra during the seasons from 1946 to 1972 gave North Carolinians a comprehensive musical experience. There were symphonies and choral works of Haydn, Bach, Mozart, and Mendelssohn; all Beethoven symphonies except No. 9; the four Brahms symphonies; concertos from Bach to Bartok; and the introduction of Scandinavian music by Alfvén, Larsson, Nielsen, and Roman. Often colorful selections from children's programs were featured for evening concerts: Villa-Lobos' *Little Train of the Caipira*; Copland's *Rodeo* and *Red Pony* suites; ballet excerpts from Stravinsky's *Petrouchka* and *Firebird*; and suites by Prokofiev and Tchaikovsky.

Choral organizations from colleges and universities were featured in a variety of choral works, and the collaborations were inspiring to the singers and the audiences. Some of the choral organizations participating with the Symphony included those from Appalachian State University, Boone; Atlantic Christian College, Wilson; Campbell College, Buies Creek; Elizabeth City State College; Elon College; High Point College; Lenoir-Rhyne College, Hickory; Mars Hill College; Saint Mary's Junior College and Peace Junior College, Raleigh; and Western Carolina University, Cullowhee.

But through the years our concerts were in no sense limited to the performance of works by great European composers. Rather, from our earliest years, when our Saturday morning rehearsals were devoted to reading new compositions by North Carolina composers, we endeavored to discover and share the best in American music. On various occasions we performed music by Copland, Gershwin, Bernstein, Hanson, Menotti, Rorem, Virgil Thomson, Griffes, Gould, Stringfield, and others. We also premiered important American works, such as the Benjamin Award pieces (see Chapter 8); Hunter Johnson's *North State*, commissioned by the Carolina Tercentenary Commission for 1963, and the new version for full orchestra of Johnson's *Letter to the World* (1960); and Alan Hovhaness's *Symphony No. 6* ("Celestial Gate"), a Benjamin Commission.

In sum, we endeavored to present a musical banquet whose varied dishes and courses would find responsive palates and awaken new sensations. We offered the great and the not-so-great, the familiar and the strange, the "comfortable" and the challenging, in our quest not merely to please but to "stretch" our listeners.

In return, the Symphony has received many heartwarming letters from the citizens of North Carolina both large and small. Among my personal favorites is the following:

> On Symphony day, I could hardly wait till 2 o'clock. I didn't know what a symphony was like and now I know. For some reason I thought I disliked music but the Symphony changed my mind . . . now when there is a concert just try to find me at home!

The Players

EVERYONE is dependent upon others in serving a common cause, attaining a common goal, and that is no less true of a symphony orchestra than it is of any other enterprise that emulates by its numbers and quality the creativity of its leadership and personnel. The sounds and skills of a symphony orchestra re-create the living concept of great music, and all are involved in the artistic purpose. A conductor may have the design in his head, but it requires the talents, knowledge, and sensitivity of the individual performers to interpret and convey the essence of a composition.

As one distinguished musician phrased it: "An orchestra is not there to provide satisfaction for the ego of its conductor, nor is it present to further the proprietary interests of the board of trustees. But the orchestra is there to create and interpret the musical logic; and only then can it function at the highest level as it conveys the beauties of a glorious sound."

In our orchestra's early years, the problem of continuing personnel was a real one. Our Full Symphony, which toured in April and May, was a fine orchestra comprising musicians from some of the best orchestras in the nation. But our prospects of securing exemplary personnel diminished gradually as other orchestras' seasons were extended due to their obtaining federal and state grants. Obtaining musicians for the Little Symphony season of January through March became very much of a problem—logically enough, given the modest salary, truncated season, and slender prospects of permanency.

It was this progressive shortage of capable personnel to fit into our touring schedule that led me to campaign more and more vigorously for a longer season. And when sufficient funds were finally available, in 1967, we restructured our schedule so that all the musicians were engaged for the entire season (as I have related in Chapter 11). Among other advantages of the new format was that it opened the possibility of interspersing Full Symphony concerts in the Little Symphony portion of the schedule.

S E R I O U S music, as I see it, is a language in itself, an *international* language and a source of inspiration and learning. While Maxine and I were visiting Guatemala in the summer of 1968, I was invited by chance to conduct a selection at a rehearsal of the Guatemala Symphony Orchestra. As a result, during our few days in Guatemala City we were greeted on the street by orchestra members who wanted to know about the United States and its music. An interesting musical evening followed, and a luncheon was arranged also at which we heard a six-year-old violin prodigy who had been trained by his father. Later that little boy entered the Durham, North Carolina, schools while his father became a leading member of the North Carolina Symphony Orchestra's violin section. After his return to Guatemala, the father, Enrique Raudales, became director of the Music Conservatory in Guatemala City.

Earlier the Symphony had initiated an international project by inviting two advanced foreign string players to spend a season with us as guest players, so that we might learn from them and they might learn from us. As a result of the success of that venture, musicians came to us eventually from Japan, Australia, Canada, Germany, South Korea, and Colombia. It was invariably a pleasure to work with them, and our audiences admired them. We regarded it as a special privilege to know such talented people from other countries.

Two young ladies from Japan who came to us were well-trained violinists, and were welcome guests in our orchestra. They seldom spoke, they dressed impeccably, and they were excellent musicians.

I inquired of one of them how old she was when she commenced her violin studies.

"Four years," she told me.

Then I asked the other one a similar question.

"Almost four," was her reply.

We also heard young children from the Suzuki group from Japan, and among them was a five-year-old violinist who played remarkably. I was told that she had begun her studies when she was two years old!

These young people reinforced my belief that if one desires to succeed in certain areas of knowledge, that desire should be inculcated early. Thus it is with our work ethic in education and specific skills such as mathematics, music, language, ballet, and athletics: it is essential to begin early, study seriously, and maintain adequate discipline.

Another talented foreign guest artist with our symphony orchestra was Kenji Kobayashi, a Japanese violinist who had been in America for some time studying at the Juilliard School of Music and who served as our concert-master in 1966.

Whenever Kenji was featured as a soloist, he became a favorite with audiences. One year just before the orchestra was leaving New Bern for Morehead City, where Kenji was to appear as soloist, he notified us that he was ill. A doctor diagnosed the illness as flu and indicated that Kenji would require two or three days of bed rest. That night I called Kenji by long distance.

"I'm recovering all right," he assured me. "But my heart's beating too fast."

"How do you know that?" I asked.

"Because I time it with the beat of my metronome," he said.

Kenji was an inveterate camera devotee. One time in Jacksonville, North Carolina, he placed his camera on a shelf by a restaurant table. When he reached the loading zone for the Symphony bus, he realized that he had forgotten his camera. The shock of this realization prevented him from climbing promptly into the bus, and Mac, our driver, playfully started moving the bus without him. We drove a short distance while Kenji ran behind in an attempt to overtake us. Then Mac stopped the bus, and Kenji came aboard and explained his problem.

Jocularly, Mac told Kenji that because of the one-way street system, driving back to town would be an added burden, and for the trouble caused, he would be forced to charge Kenji one dollar. That night Mac found in his hotel mailbox a letter with one dollar enclosed and a note from Kenji in Japanese script. The script was so artistic that Mac later furnished Kenji with a brush and black paint with which to decorate the walls of a motel restaurant in Morganton. And year after year upon our returning to that restaurant, the proprietors invariably inquired about Kenji.

Later, in 1974, while Maxine and I were in Tokyo, Kenji came to our hotel to visit us. He brought with him three Japanese professors of music and he served as interpreter for an engrossing discussion. Now Kenji has a family and is concert-master of the Metropolitan Orchestra of Tokyo. Our international project, we regret, was later discontinued by the new administration.

On turning on my radio one day, I heard Mozart's *Piano Sonata No. 14 in C Minor* being played in a dull and unimaginative manner. I was curious to know the identity of the pianist, but at the close of the sonata there was no announcement of the artist, merely the statement: "Now we move from Mozart's *Symphony No. 40* to *Symphony No. 41.*"

So I telephoned the station to ask who the soloist was in the previous selection, and to say there was evidently an error in the program notes because the announcer had called it a "symphony." A boyish voice replied that the selection was a *cantata* by Mozart. I said that was still a mistake, because the selection was not a choral work but a sonata for piano.

"Well, I don't know nothin' about classical music," he answered, "and I'm just fillin' in for a guy who's sick. But the label on the record says this piece is in three parts, and it's by Moe-zart."

After hearing that colorless performance, I could understand why

Leonard Bernstein once announced at a concert in which a musician whose name I shall not mention was to perform Brahms's *Piano Concerto No. 1* with the New York Philharmonic, that he would eschew responsibility for the interpretation of the work! (I have been told, however, that even though the conductor and the soloist had widely differing ideas about the interpretation, the performance came off well and the conductor and the soloist remained good friends.)

In the wide world of music as in other arts, I have come to appreciate the fact that I have no right to say or believe that *my* interpretation of any work—music, writing, painting, sculpture, whatever—is the only legitimate interpretation, the only defensible one. Composers, conductors, performing musicians, authors, book reviewers, dramatists, producers, drama critics who sit on the aisle seats at opening-night performances—all have their rights of opinion. And I am pleased that generally, and often emphatically, they freely exercise these rights.

The concept of the importance of "stars" in music, for American audiences, is often that of hearing favorite artists with little concern for what they play or sing. The European is just as eager to enjoy the superlative artist, but his tradition has been to place the emphasis upon the music itself. As someone phrased it, "You don't need the 'stars' and they don't need you."

The North Carolina Symphony through the years has been fortunate in being able to present stars and visiting conductors, but it was invariably a problem of logistics for us to arrange when and where a soloist might rehearse because of the intensive travel, and still further complications had to be resolved in reserving a special rehearsal time for a guest conductor.

We had quite a number of invited soloists during the early years, including Leslie Parnas, Gayle Smith, and Phyllis Kraeuter, 'cellists; violinists Georgio Ciompi, Carroll Glenn, Karl Kraeuter, Sergio Luca, Setsuko Nagata, Ruggiero Ricci, Elaine Skorodin, Tossy Spivakovsky, and Mari Tsumura; pianists Edward Cone, Harold Cone, Daniel Ericourt, Egon Petri, and Paul Stassevitch; and vocalists

Helen Boatwright, Norman Cordon, Jerome Hines, Malcolm Smith, and Eleanor Steber.

I particularly recall among members of the orchestra who have performed as soloists at concerts a fine violist, Janée Gilbert. She soon inquired if her fiancé Lorne Monroe, a Canadian, might be invited to play a 'cello concerto. We knew that his schooling and experience were exceptional. He was a pupil of the late great 'cellist Gregor Piatigorsky at the Curtis Institute of Music, and we were pleased to welcome him as soloist.

Soon afterward, the couple married. Lorne's career has been as solo 'cellist with the Philadelphia Orchestra and presently with the New York Philharmonic. The two indeed have had productive careers. Years after they played in our orchestra I was happy to meet Lorne backstage in New York.

"How is Janée?" was the first question I asked him, and "How many sons do you have now?" was the next.

"Ten sons and one daughter," he said, and he was smiling broadly.

There was another 'cellist, Daniel Domb, whom we enjoyed having as soloist from time to time, and the audiences responded enthusiastically to his artistry. He would carry on conversations with the players and relate interesting experiences he had had in teaching. One story was especially amusing: One of his 'cello students, he said, played badly and had unattractive mannerisms, so Domb in an effort to point out to the student the absurd errors he was making, resorted to mimicking the student's manner of playing. Whereupon, the student responded in a huff: "But that is exactly the way I played it!"

At the close of each Symphony season, we realized that many of our friends with whom we had enjoyed inspired music-making we might never see again. Perhaps they were looking ahead to teaching or other duties, to further study in colleges and conservatories, to travel abroad, or to employment with other orchestras offering higher remuneration and lighter travel schedules. Of course, our favorite players were generally those who returned year after year because of the persuasion that sharing their talents through pro-

With some of my favorite players: Beth Sears, Beatrice Griffin,
Christian Kutschinski, and Gary DeLeon
(Courtesy of the North Carolina Department of Archives and History)

grams played in the hamlets as well as the cities of North Carolina constituted a mission.

Outstanding among those musical missionaries who were prominent in reaching audiences was Major Christian Kutschinski, violist, who had been chairman of the music department at North Carolina State University for many years. After retiring from his duties at that institution, he was freer to undertake tours with the North Carolina Symphony. Such a human spirit is unusual in the competitive musical marketplace—he was a fine gentleman, a versatile musician, a teacher, and a friend.

Beth Sears, oboist, a former student of the French oboist Marcel Tabuteau (of the Philadelphia Orchestra), learned from the master how to phrase and enlarge her musicianship. She played with the North Carolina Symphony for thirteen years, after which she became a researcher in the music division of the Library of Congress. Her plans for retirement were fulfilled by building an attractive home in Sun City, Arizona, where she now lives with Crystal Gut-heil, a former violinist with us and with the National Symphony.

Gary DeLeon, tympanist, was also with us for many years, and he is another alumnus of the orchestra whose musicianship I remember happily and appreciate. Among our other performers I recall particularly Richard Andrews and Raymond Wood, double bassists with the San Antonio and Baltimore Symphony Orchestras, respectively; Edamay McCulley, violinist; Donald Peck, first flutist, now with the Chicago Symphony; and Gilbert Johnson, now first trumpeter with the Philadelphia Orchestra.

These performers and many others brought distinction to our musical aggregation. On many occasions there were deep personal attachments, and the spirit of good music quickened our efforts for both the children and the adult audiences. There lingered memories of some wonderful music and wonderful friends.

To quote that master-artist with words, William Shakespeare, from Act II, Scene 7, of *As You Like It*:

> All the world's a stage,
> And all the men and women merely players:
> They have their exits and their entrances;
> And one man in his time plays many parts,
> His acts being seven ages.

I N D I V I D U A L members of the orchestra sometimes had particular difficulties with personal problems. One member disappeared prior to a rehearsal and left us this note:

> By now, you probably know I've run away. . . . You have been especially good this year and I hope your tour is a success. . . . Know that I will be all right. I will write you as soon as I can, as to where and how I am.

We had an idea where that individual was headed. We telephoned to bus stations along his probable route and located the suffering one, and he agreed to return the following morning.

Rooming assignments were no problem in the case of married couples. But sometimes the personnel manager ran into difficulties in the pairing of other orchestra personnel. One girl from the Far West was accustomed to sleeping with wide-open windows, and it was torture for her to adjust to her roommate's preference for having little outside ventilation—so the personnel manager tried whenever possible to assign her a single room. But whenever this was done for any one individual, it naturally opened Pandora's box. All had their rights, and some were not reluctant to declare them. Oboists, of course, were assigned single rooms to permit them the freedom to make reeds for their delicate instruments.

Beatrice Griffin, our leading violinist for several years, had become accustomed to performing in unheated buildings in Sweden during the war, and she thus had some difficulty in adjusting to America's overheated hotels and auditoriums. Even the Symphony's bus was too warm for her during our midwinter touring. Beatrice never showed impatience, however, or irritability, and her friendliness was evident even to members of the audience. Frequently she attended after-concert parties, where she was welcomed by concert-goers who were anticipating her presence. Her playing was equally impressive, for her violin tone was succulent, the execution extremely facile, and her artistic taste was impeccable.

O U R musical missionaries of earlier days had performed at orthopedic, mental, and veterans' hospitals, at the state prison, at Camp Butner, and at other institutions—and it was done gladly, as part of the job. There was no thought that because such concerts were "difficult," there should be increased remuneration for presenting them. But as time went on, we began to notice a change of attitude among the musicians of our orchestra. On one occasion, a player requested a modest supplement for "doubling" on the triangle. The conductor had invited him to move forward to the outside of the stage in a rural community so that the children could see him play the brief triangle part; the musician complied, but at the conclusion of the matinee he requested a raise because he had functioned as a "soloist."

On another occasion we played the *Toy Symphony* of Haydn for our children's audiences on tour. Immediately prior to a radio broadcast, one of the players who doubled on percussion refused to perform a small part for the toy trumpet unless he could be assured a salary increase. Had we granted his request, it would have generated other changes and other problems with the musicians who *volunteered* to play short passages with blocks, rattles, and other unconventional, nonmusical instruments during the *Toy Symphony*.

When our second oboist became ill just before a concert, the conductor asked the principal oboist to cue in a few notes from a second oboe passage. The curt reply from the principal oboist was that he would not play a lower part or fill in for a second oboist because he was a *principal*. I oppose un-American class distinctions in our orchestras, such as principal, co-principal, associate principal, assistant principal, and so on. Surely all parts must be played, and each musician should be qualified to perform whether it is a contra-bassoon part or a second violin part. America is a great egalitarian society. Let us have great music!

Such experiences pointed up the need for precaution in the drafting of master contracts for the musicians. How should one define an orchestral "solo"? Should that concept cover a single phrase, or the demonstration of an instrument at a children's concert?

Gunther Schuller in the June 1980 *High Fidelity Magazine* wrote of another problem besetting today's professional musicians, in an article entitled "The Trouble with Orchestras." His theme was that "joy" has disappeared from the faces of many professional musicians. As a result, he contended, musicians have become bored and some may even detest music. This sad situation, he said, has been the result in part of a "union mentality," with more concern about time, rehearsals, and increasing financial gains along with decreasing effort.

There is some validity in this point of view; it seems that some American orchestras have reduced their rehearsals to three per week regardless of the difficulties of their programs. Naturally musicians can list a "catalog of evils" relating to the "tyrannization" by conductors who once possessed unquestioned control, although that has now changed. Schuller also cited what he considers "natural enemies" of musicians, such as boards of trustees, executive committees, and incompetent managers, resulting in adversary relationships.

One unfortunate development in American orchestras is that administration is sometimes dominated by amateurs. Business men and women generally have only a limited understanding of the administration relating to an artistic enterprise, where ideals and sacrifices and the quest of artistic perfection are essential.

The commercial profession of music can be a hard and uncertain business. One musician expressed it well: "I attended a midnight union meeting in New York, and after that experience, I was ready to give up a musical career." Some people may be shocked to learn that orchestra musicians can exchange tuxedos for "hard hats" as they threaten strikes. During the 1970–71 season, for example, the Minnesota Orchestra was on stage formally dressed for a performance, but the seated musicians remained silent. They refused to play, because they were on strike! It was an effective protest; the orchestra clearly conveyed its message to the audience.

What people generally tend to forget is that musicians often feel insecure, and build a defense between themselves and the conductor or administration. I surmise that the apprehensions about conductors are but another manifestation of capital versus labor. While music is a great art, it is also for musicians a compulsion and a somewhat precarious profession. However, musicians who are mature and experienced are indispensable in a professional orchestra.

Sometimes, of course, musicians may be lacking in appreciation and tact, and every conductor should anticipate such problems during rehearsals and be prepared to deal with them along with admonishing his players about such things as excessive conversation and careless stage dress and manners. The ego and selfishness that beset all of us sometimes can be repugnant within a group. I recall that several years ago there was being promoted what was called a "hate" program against a well-known conductor. It was said that whenever that orchestra visited a certain city, there was an after-concert hotel party designated as a "hate-the-conductor" festivity. Perhaps it had a background of levity, but the point was obvious.

It seems inevitable that there will be conflicts among the personnel of a symphonic orchestra. Each individual wants something and his wants may become "multipliers." (As Schopenhauer once declared, desire leads to cupidity and avarice.)

In the case of our orchestra, a new dimension developed rather precipitately in 1970. Just before Christmas, I learned that the national office of the American Federation of Musicians had encouraged the formation of orchestra committees for symphony orchestras. They were ostensibly to be elected by orchestra members themselves and to become semi-autonomous agencies. And they were to formulate demands against orchestral administrations for higher salaries, longer seasons, shorter working hours, restrictions on travel, and other so-called rights.

One day a small group of musicians asked me to have lunch with them, and I suggested that they also ask the personnel manager. But, they declared, they wanted to talk *with me*. They asked me if I were agreeable to the formation of an orchestra committee. I told them that in my opinion the formation of such a committee could be a good thing, *if* the committee were maintained on a cooperative basis and if "hotheads" did not assume control of it.

But the hotheads did assume control, and the committee became truculent, especially in the spring of 1971, at a time when university centers were being harassed by protesters and dissenters. It was also at the point when the North Carolina Symphony organization was involved in working for the Ford Challenge Campaign. The musicians anticipated immediate salary raises, lighter travel and concert schedules with longer seasons, and other perquisites. Meanwhile, I was not able to be on tour constantly because of fund-raising activities, although I rehearsed and conducted many of the scheduled evening concerts.

In personnel policies, I believe, there should be a grievance committee comprising perhaps two members from the trustees, two from the local American Federation of Musicians, one labor attorney, and two members of the orchestra. This I had recommended to the executive committee and board in 1971, and it was to function for labor and management—in other words, in both directions.

In 1971, however, the General Assembly did not complete its biennial appropriation work until late in June; we were thus handicapped in planning increases to the musicians and staff, because we did not know whether we might suffer a reduction in our legislative request. In light of this situation, our administrative staff in March sent the members of the orchestra this notice:

> Due to the uncertainty of the financial picture of the North Carolina Symphony Orchestra with regard to the future season, we are at present able to issue only a limited number of contracts (primarily strings) for the 1971–72 season.
>
> Although symphony orchestras generally face critical financial difficulties, it is particularly acute for the North Carolina Symphony at the moment because the General Assembly of the State of North Carolina has not yet approved the Appropriations Bill for the biennium 1971–73. Although the Symphony Society is not a State agency, a substantial share of our operating funds comes from the State, and we must be extremely careful in making financial commitments. A recent public announcement indicated that *financial requests* already being debated exceeded the State's anticipated income by some $683,000,000.
>
> The Ford Foundation's program of aid to symphony orchestras ends on June 30, 1971. Should we not match our challenge grant from the Foundation, there will be a further loss of some $35,000 in annual interest.
>
> In view of this, each musician who does not receive a renewal of contract by the North Carolina Symphony Society by March 31, 1971, is obviously free to secure other employment upon expiration of the current contract, April 30, 1971.
>
> Many thanks for your work and interest and best wishes always.
>
> Yours sincerely,
Hiram B. Black
Manager

Resentment on the part of the musicians whose contracts had not been renewed may have caused some members of the orchestra to make inquiries of the American Federation of Musicians in New York. Encouraged by its dictates and policies, along with the practices of some metropolitan orchestras—orchestras with budgets from $500,000 to $1,000,000, as designated by the American Symphony Orchestra League—it appears that they may have been in consultation with an attorney from the Teamsters' Union of New York.

When there were threats of a walkout or strike, Russell Olsen, president of Local No. 500, A.F. of M. in Raleigh, sent this telegram (April 1, 1971):

Local No. 500 A.F. of M. wishes to state its position both for the musicians and for the North Carolina Symphony.
   (1) The North Carolina Symphony reserves its freedom of contract just as each individual reserves the right to freedom of contract. This must be maintained.
   (2) All contracts terminate April 30, 1971, and therefore, there is no further obligation to any party, and each person is free to negotiate with other individuals and organizations. There is no automatic renewal of any kind to any of the employees of the North Carolina Symphony.
   (3) A walkout on the part of the Orchestra Committee has no Union approval. It cannot be condoned by the Local No. 500 A.F. of M. which I represent. It also could result in dismissal of any individual concerned. And offers of contract relative to the proposed contract for the 1971–72 season may be cancellable for any members participating in such a "wildcat" walkout. I also may file formal charges of breach of contract. In the event of an illicit walkout or an impairment of the Symphony program, each offending member will be reported to his own local and may be subject to damages due to the loss of income.
Suggestions which you have for next season must never result in impairment of present contract that requires each member to do

his best and cooperate for fine performances. We are all obligated to the public, and we must have assurance from you by Saturday, April 3, 1971, that you will maintain your contractual agreement in good faith for the best interest of all. Please wire.

As it turned out, we did not suffer a reduction in our legislative appropriation and our 1971–72 season (my last) was able to proceed with a full complement of players.

W E of the Symphony Society honor the dedication and skills of the North Carolina Symphony members over the years, for they have participated in building a "cathedral of sound within a cosmos." We offer our gratitude for their contribution to our musical experiences.

A Culmination

The Ford Grant

FROM its beginning, the North Carolina Symphony Orchestra followed the policy of paying all bills promptly. We knew that "an empty bag cannot stand upright," as Benjamin Franklin once declared, and board members and friends helped with suggestions as to how we might assemble a savings package for a reserve fund. The story of our efforts fills these pages. No matter how hard we worked, our treasury was never overflowing; our income was always uncertain.

One day in the fall of 1965 I called on Alan Rich, the music editor of a large newspaper in New York. This was during one of my annual visits to New York and other large cities to hold auditions for capable musicians, especially for those who could be available at the beginning of our orchestra season in January. During such visits I customarily talked with teachers and with various foundations, including the Ford Foundation of New York. In 1965 I had already been to the Ford Foundation office when I stopped in to give Mr. Rich a news release detailing the record of our past season and the projected schedule for the new season.

"Are you getting in on the Ford windfall?" he asked me, the moment I walked in. I told him I had just come from the office of the Ford Foundation, but I had heard nothing of any windfall.

"Well, the Foundation has projected a gift of $81,000,000 to some sixty symphony orchestras in the United States," Mr. Rich said, "and I suggest that you communicate with them *immediately*. An announcement will be made about it this coming Friday in the *New York Times*."

I was perturbed when I checked with an acquaintance in the Foundation and was told that the North Carolina Symphony Orchestra was not included in the list of recipients. I called Maxine in Chapel Hill, and from then on, even during the remainder of my auditions in other cities and colleges, our campaign for recognition was under way.

A couple of days after talking with Mr. Rich I went to Boston to continue my auditions, and early the following Friday I had a telephone call from Paul Green.

"Have you seen the *New York Times* this morning?" Paul asked.

"No, but I know what's in it," I told him, "and I am sick about it!"

My auditions trip took me on to other colleges. When I returned to Chapel Hill, Christmas was approaching, and there was no apparent hope of a windfall from Ford.

But early one morning in 1966, several weeks later, I had a telephone call from New York, and a mysterious voice inquired if I had received any messages from the Ford Foundation during the last several days. When I explained that I hadn't, he said he had been trying during the entire weekend to get in touch with me. He then asked, "Could you come to New York next Tuesday, January 18, for a two-thirty meeting at the Foundation offices?" I might invite someone to come with me, he said, or I could come alone.

I made an effort to secure the company of the president of the Symphony Society, or one of the other officers, but they were unavailable. Then I got in touch with the Honorable Victor S. Bryant of Durham, who had served previously as the Society's president. Mr. Bryant assured me he would accompany me, and I was thrilled!

At the Ford Foundation offices a gentleman whom I had met in Chicago some years before greeted us cordially. It appeared that he had been familiar with my work (and struggles) for several years, and to some extent this alleviated my stage fright. After the preliminary handshaking, Mr. Bryant and I and several representatives from the Ford Foundation, including one distinguished lady, went into the conference room, which was equipped with several microphones. The first question asked me was based upon information that we had submitted earlier relating to orchestra personnel:

"Is Miss X"—the questioner gave her name—"a good violist?"

"Yes," I replied.

"Why would she come down to play for you in North Carolina for that salary?"

"I do not know," I answered, "except that she *wanted* to come; and then, too, her teacher at the University of Michigan has maintained an interest in the work that we seek to achieve."

And so the interrogation went on.

"Where is your rehearsal hall?"

"*Anywhere*," I said. "In a gymnasium, school auditorium, or church." This seemed incomprehensible, and someone, with a bit of sarcasm, asked:

"Haven't you ever heard of Carnegie Hall, or Orchestra Hall in Chicago?"

I assured him I had heard of both.

I recall that Victor Bryant had expected the meeting at the Foundation to be a brief one. He and his wife wished to do some shopping for furniture, but they were unable to do so because the meeting lasted two and one-half hours. And it was the most austere confrontation I had ever endured. When the meeting concluded, Mr. Bryant commented: "Mrs. Thompson and gentlemen: This has been impossible, but *it has been done.*" And evidently referring to the Apostle Paul's admonition, he added: "Be thou not weary of thy good works." Then the meeting adjourned, Mr. Bryant went his way, and I returned to Chapel Hill.

From that point on, the correspondence with the Foundation became more frequent, and I was gratified to observe a new confidence and a feeling that enabled us to hold our heads high, even though at that point we scarcely dared to discuss the Ford Foundation matter with anyone.

I continued to ponder the questions asked and the suggestions

Receiving our honorary degrees from Duke University President Terry Sanford,
while Trustee Mary Duke Biddle Semans looks on
(Photo by Duke University Photography Department)

offered at the meeting. Those suggestions included the following: a
season of four months is inadequate; the ratio of rehearsals to performances is inequitable; the salaries of the musicians must be up-
graded; a thinner distribution of concerts is essential; the working
conditions of the players could be subject to examination; a home
base for the orchestra is imperative; the racial policy should be
defined; a plan for increasing employment for musicians is needed;
the program should be a realistic one, even though the present plan
is "interesting"; and the orchestra should not become a "traveling
show."

While we were waiting to hear from the Foundation—a tense
period indeed—there was a host of things to do: detailed forms to
fill out for the Foundation, reports relating to the occupations
of members of the board of trustees, lists of personnel for the past
five years, budgets for five years, "tickets" sold, corporate gifts,
weekly salaries, working conditions, schedules, and programs. And

to judge the orchestra's musical quality, the Foundation desired tapes of actual concerts. I recall one in particular that we mailed to them, that of a broadcast in which the Stravinsky *Firebird Suite* concluded the program. In all, some ten pounds of reports, we estimated, were sent to the Foundation. Much of the work had to be prepared on tour late at night following concerts, and by long-distance calls to the Symphony office in Chapel Hill. But our fulfillment of the requirements was punctual and adequate.

Subsequent requests were to enlarge a plan for our sustaining fund, or maintenance fund, and to submit a ten-year plan for the orchestra. We were then encouraged to believe that the authorities were examining our project favorably.

I recall that it seemed difficult to convince the Symphony trustees of the enormity of the project that might be ahead. However, a statement from a board member, Mrs. Norris Hodgkins, Jr., at one of the board meetings, was encouraging:

> I was thrilled when I had the opportunity to read the projected ten-year plan for the North Carolina Symphony Orchestra. My reaction was similar to the feeling that I had twenty-one years ago when I heard the orchestra for the first time. This was the beginning of something new, something unique, something very special, led by our very own talented and competent pioneer, Dr. Swalin. You know the record compiled by our state orchestra in the last twenty-one seasons and it is a record in which the entire state can take pride. Now Dr. Swalin has done it again. He has, through this projected ten-year report, given us a challenge, a dream, a vision of what can be done.
>
> These are just a few highlights of the plan, which seeks to insure continued quality, extends fine music to a great audience, and attracts talented young people to professional careers. Meanwhile, I believe it will attract additional financial support for the orchestra.
>
> Mr. President, in short, let's stop talking and proceed with this excellent plan for a bigger and better North Carolina Symphony.

In February 1966 the president of the Symphony Society, state senator Voit Gilmore, at a board meeting generously praised our work: "It seems to me that the office staff and Ben have been doing this by themselves," he observed. "It is quite an achievement."

Our office staff was a "family," with each member contributing his or her best skills toward achieving the Ford challenge. When our barracks-office was propped up to be removed from the campus, the staff worked long hours to organize and label materials to be moved to the future trailer offices. And when the Swalins' screened porch served as a temporary office, no one complained about the extra driving or the heat of the porch. A particular heroine during this period was our office manager, Miss Helen Reinhardt, who became budget officer and then secretary-treasurer of the Society—in effect, the controller of Symphony affairs. Her maintenance of the accounts and records was meticulous, and her relationship with the State Auditor's office was exemplary. Unfortunately for the Society, Miss Reinhardt was compelled to resign in 1972 when the administration of the Symphony was reshaped.

Another colleague whose service was of the highest quality and importance was our executive secretary, Mrs. Tempe Newsome Prouty. Her resignation followed shortly that of Miss Reinhardt. Throughout her years of superlative skill Mrs. Prouty displayed unflinching loyalty, and she remains a cherished friend.

O u r suspense came to an end in June.

Helen Reinhardt was on the porch frantically waving a letter and shouting, "It's here! It's here!" Quickly we gathered around to hear the news from the Ford Foundation that we had been anticipating so eagerly. "I am pleased to inform you," the letter from Joseph M. McDaniel, Jr. (secretary of the Ford Foundation), began, "that the Ford Foundation has approved a grant of $1,000,000 to the North Carolina Symphony Society, Inc., subject to the conditions set forth herein. . . ." It was an exhilirating moment, and our group impulse was to share it with everyone! One million dollars! One M I L L I O N dollars! But the letter contained a caution that it was too early to shout the good news: "The Foundation will refer to this grant at a later date in a press release that will be sent you in advance. *No* prior announcement should be made by the Orchestra. If you wish to release additional information thereafter or as an addendum to the Foundation's release, you are free to do so without prior clearance from us."

The ultimate press release read as follows:

> A grant of one million dollars to the North Carolina Symphony from the Ford Foundation was announced today by Governor Moore, by the Society President, Voit Gilmore, and Symphony director, Benjamin Swalin. Under the terms of the grant as revealed by the Foundation, $250,000 is an outright gift to the orchestra to be paid in annual installments of $50,000, while the other portion, $750,000, is a challenge grant to be raised from private sources by the North Carolina Symphony Society over a five-year period, through June 30, 1971.

It was a period of jubilation for us, representing a new phase of achievement. Senator Gilmore, thrilled as all of us were, appreciated the newly attained situation and appraised it accurately, if laconically, when he said to me: "Ben, you will have many new friends now."

There were, of course, numerous other observations and comments, including this one from Dr. Robert Lee Humber: "I think it was a bright moment in the history of the North Carolina Symphony Society when the Ford Foundation was willing to offer the challenge, and I believe the goal is realistic, and we should go for *three* million dollars, definitely stating that the Ford Foundation has already subscribed to one million, in the appeal to the people of the state." (The figure of three million was proposed to include one million as a reserve fund.)

The million-dollar grant gave almost immediate recognition to the orchestra's stature in the state, the leadership of the administration, the board of trustees, and to others who had devoted their time and talents to the Symphony over the years. The munificent grant was based upon a review of the orchestra's artistic quality, the scope and diversity of its activities, the stability and continuity of its operations, and other characteristics. But it was also a challenge; we must not merely maintain the quality of performance and repertoire, with services to our young audiences and the community chapters, we must also project a realistic vision for the coming decade.

Until the Ford Foundation allocated its magnanimous dispensation of approximately $81,000,000 in grants to selected American orchestras in June 1966, there was little encouragement for real expansion of many orchestras. The Foundation was indeed perceptive in its aim to assist the orchestras in augmenting the salaries of musicians, and to improve the working conditions of orchestra personnel, along with other basic needs. We were profoundly grateful for their interest and aid to the North Carolina Symphony.

The Ford Foundation's conditions for matching the challenge grant represented a masterful plan. As one of the qualifying orchestras, we were given $50,000 in "expendable" funds for each of five years of the program to defray the administrative costs of achieving the matching grant. In addition, we were required to raise an annual sustaining fund of $42,500—a figure calculated by the Foundation from the information we had given them on our non-earned non-state income. (The sustaining fund was not to be counted as part of the grant-matching total.)

The precise terms of the challenge were as follows:

1. That the Endowment Funds, which shall be held in a Trust established by the Ford Foundation for a period of ten years, should be matched by the Orchestra within the five-year period July 1, 1966, through June 30, 1971, through contributions from sources other than the Foundation amounting to one dollar for each Endowment dollar granted by the Foundation.

2. That the Orchestra shall continue its regular operations and shall not suspend its activities for a significant period of time during the ten-year period of the program, July 1, 1966, through June 30, 1976.

3. That funds raised by the Orchestra in its annual maintenance or sustaining drives during the first five years of the program will not be less than $42,500 per year.
4. That non-restrictive practices with regard to audiences at public concerts and non-discriminatory personnel practices inclusive of open auditions are observed by the Orchestra.
5. That the Orchestra is exempt from Federal income taxes under the provision of Section 501 . . . of the Internal Revenue Code.

A fund-raising organization from New York was employed in December 1966; unfortunately, however, that group proved ineffective, except for one lady who worked faithfully but who was soon transferred to another assignment. I was on tour with the orchestra, and I was obviously concerned when the fund-raising appeared to be inadequate. I received protests from trustees and others who had granted appointments that were not fulfilled by representatives of the organization's staff. Our ultimate goal of $3,000,000 now seemed light-years away.

During the five-year challenge period (1966–71), we realized, we must also face operating deficits. The budget as of February 1967 was a little more than $300,000; but our expansion would augment the level of expenditures to approximately $500,000 by 1971. During that period, we knew that our income would have to be increased on all fronts: state appropriations, memberships, corporate gifts, and individual contributions.

Since I had turned over the administration and responsibility of the Ford drive to a committee from the Symphony board, there appeared to have been some grievous errors in the conduct of the campaign, one of which was the inordinate delay in obtaining a Symphony drive chairman.

In April 1968 the board gave a campaign luncheon to announce the opening of the Ford Challenge Campaign. But there was still no drive chairman! The committee had anticipated securing U.S. District Judge Richardson Preyer of Greensboro as chairman. When he declined, the committee approached his charming wife, Emily. Although she graciously accepted the chairmanship, her service essentially would be lending her good name and prestige, because she would have limited time for the onerous business of organizing committees, money-raising, and travel. In any event, a disconnected organization resulted and I became uneasy. I realized that the chairmanship problem should have been resolved many months earlier.

After discontinuing the fund-raising services of the New York company, the trustees favored employing a North Carolinian who would be acquainted with the state's resources and its citizens. The man they selected began the task with high hopes, but he soon cast his eyes in another direction rather than toward the burdensome task of raising funds. The monthly income from his efforts proved to be less than the salary involved, and the treasurer affirmed that there was little justification for continuing the relationship. The employee's resignation was approved in March 1970.

As a result of that experience, the trustees concluded that any new person engaged to complete the drive would represent an unknown quantity, and in the final analysis the responsibility was that of the board. Because the laity must also be identified with the fund-raising effort, and because my identity had been established with the Symphony, the trustees then decided that "Ben Swalin should become the 'focal point' for the campaign." They expressed concern about the need for adequate assistance, and requested that a plan be drawn up to carry the drive to a conclusion.

During this time of giving deep thought to our situation, I was also seeking the advice of specialists, not only for drawing up a workable plan, but also for my problem of having to wear too many hats. An experienced, able gentleman from a midwestern university flew down to grant me valuable counsel: "Never become known as a fund-raiser," he cautioned. "You are a professional man with an established image, and you must maintain contact with the orchestra and the public, even though your appearances might be diminished. Get loyal assistance for some of the conducting, and loyal assistance in the office."

R E V E L A T I O N of the new direction the campaign would be taking was made in a letter of May 15, 1970, from then-President William Westphal of the North Carolina Symphony Society to the Society's trustees. "Upon the authority granted to the Executive Committee," he announced, "Dr. Swalin has been appointed to head the Development Program to promote the Ford Foundation Challenge Campaign, and a plan has been evolved by Dr. Swalin with the concurrence of the officers and the approval of the Executive Committee for the further prosecution of the Ford Foundation Campaign. . . ."

Our master plan accentuated concentrating upon obtaining large gifts from foundations, industries, trustees, and community leaders, with participation by the governor of North Carolina. Trustees responded with their own contributions and solicitations, and the Symphony staff itself was remarkably cooperative.

At this time the notion of establishing a home base for the Symphony was being talked about. Some members of Raleigh's Chamber of Commerce envisioned the capital city as a proper location, and I was invited to be a guest at a Chamber business meeting. I urged the members at the meeting to assist us in raising $1,000,000 toward the Ford Foundation challenge grant, but their enthusiasm appeared to diminish when they realized that a fund-raising project of such dimensions would become a sine qua non. The Chamber did designate one of its members to assist with the project, but the response he encountered was disappointing and he discontinued his efforts.

When I spoke with Governor Robert Scott, he declared that "We will not forfeit the Ford money." I then made it clear that we needed assistance from him, but that he should not jeopardize his political position in order to help us. The governor and Mrs. Scott did indeed assist us munificently by giving a series of dinners at the Governor's Mansion, where guests who could contribute substantially were shown a film, *A Symphony in Jeopardy*. The guests were encouraged further to learn of the merits of the project by examining a take-home packet of literature. Governor Scott also requested

Wayne Corpenning of the Wachovia Bank in Winston-Salem to assist in the drive.

Helen Reinhardt accounted accurately for every contribution to the drive and kept us informed at all times of its progress. Helpful too in assuring the success of the campaign were the transfer of Jerald Pierce from chapter work to assist in the campaign effort, and the assigning of Guilford Daugherty to be a field representative in his place.

Maxine inaugurated two special projects for raising money: Gracious hostesses throughout North Carolina responded to her "pyramid luncheons" program by initiating luncheons for six contributing guests who in turn became hostesses; that project yielded $25,899.53. For the other project, Maxine encouraged children to contribute by dropping nickels and dimes into strategically placed barrels after matinee concerts. Special permission was granted through the governor and the superintendent of public instruction in order for children to contribute, subject to local authorities. And our bus driver, Mac McAllister, was meticulous in counting the coins as part of his daily chores. By the end of the season, the children had given $7,193.

Our intense, *cooperative* efforts met with wonderful success. It was joyous news across the state when the North Carolina Symphony Society surpassed its goal of $750,000 within the deadline of June 30, 1971. The summary statement of the Ford Foundation, issued July 23, 1971, disclosed a total of $843,171!

Confirmation of this achievement was received by the North Carolina Symphony Society two months later in a letter from William H. Nims, assistant secretary of the Ford Foundation, dated September 28, 1971. The letter said, in part, "I am pleased to inform you that the committee (Ford Foundation) has determined that the North Carolina Symphony has met the conditions of the grant and, as a consequence, will continue to retain its beneficial interest in the income of the principal. . . ." In 1973 the Ford Foundation printed a summary of its Endowment Trust for Symphony Orchestras. The Ford Foundation *Letter* of February 1 confirmed that "fifty-five of the sixty orchestras that received endowment shares subsequently met or surpassed the matching requirement. . . . The principal of the trust will be distributed at the conclusion of the program in 1976. In the meantime, the orchestras will continue to receive dividends from the trust."

The shares of the five orchestras discontinued from participation in the endowment trust were re-allocated among the fifty-five other orchestras. Consequently, in 1977 the North Carolina Symphony Society received from the Ford Foundation an additional $882,153.03. When added to the matching fund of $843,171, this meant that the Symphony Society had realized a grand total of $1,725,324 from the Ford Foundation grant.

I am deeply grateful to the Ford Foundation, and to the friends and public who so magnanimously have supported our quest. In bringing our music to the people, the people themselves have spoken, and the children by this time have grown up with the North Carolina Symphony. I rejoice that the Symphony has won new recognition.

And now, reflecting upon the struggles and progress in attaining that goal, I recall the statement of the Honorable Victor Bryant at the conclusion of our interview with the Ford Foundation officials in New York on that memorable January 18, 1966: "This has been impossible, but *it has been done!*"

Epilogue

SOME day I hope to relate the many other felicities of my life in music, in North Carolina, and in the world—but this book belongs to the North Carolina Symphony. To all who have worked with Maxine and me to bring the world's great music to the people of this state, to all our companions on the hard-circus road, I shall always be grateful.

It pleases me profoundly that even today, in communities across the state, someone will occasionally stop me on the street and exclaim, "I know you! When I was in the"—he or she will specify the grade and school—"I heard the North Carolina Symphony!"

Music has moral potentialities; for through it, a student can grow from the small to the large in terms of quality of existence, character, and nobility of soul. Music is one of the great creative developments of our Western civilization. What a pleasure and a privilege it has been to share it!

Members of the Organizing Committee of the North Carolina Symphony Society

Joseph Hyde Pratt, chairman
Felix A. Grisette, secretary
Ralph Boggs
Mrs. A. C. Burnham
Jack Dungan
Robert B. House

Mrs. F. E. Lykes
Mrs. Joseph Pratt
Mr. and Mrs. John Powell
Mr. and Mrs. Lamar Stringfield
Tyre C. Taylor

Announcement of the Federal Emergency Relief Administration Project

BECAUSE many musicians in North Carolina are in distressing circumstances, the Federal Emergency Relief Administration decided to make this symphony orchestra a relief project. This action was part of a general plan for musicians throughout the country, whose economic condition had been seriously impaired by the introduction of sound moving pictures and mechanically reproduced music.

The North Carolina Symphony Society was the natural agency to supervise the distribution of musician relief in this State because its Directors were in close touch with all the musicians and were familiar with their financial circumstances.

In May of this year [1934], an allotment of funds was authorized sufficient to pay sixty-five musicians moderate salaries for a period of eight months. The authorization includes no provision for transportation, rental of auditoriums, etc. It is, therefore, necessary to charge admission to the concerts to defray these incidental costs.

It is the sincere hope of the Federal Relief Administration, as well as of the officers and Directors of the Symphony Society, that this movement can be made into a permanent self-sustaining project so that the members of the orchestra's personnel will become self-supporting, and so that North Carolina may retain this State-wide orchestra as a focal point for the efforts of its musicians.

Presidents of the North Carolina Symphony Society (1932–73)

Col. Joseph Hyde Pratt	1932–42
Mrs. Charles E. Johnson	1942–43
Harry Fulcher Comer	1943–45
Spencer Murphy	1946–49
Charles E. Jordan	1949–55
Russell M. Grumman	1956–58
M. Elliott Carroll	1959–60
Mrs. C. B. Jefferson (Mrs. Carl Durham)	
(Acting President)	1961
Hon. James McClure Clarke	1962–63
Hon. Victor S. Bryant	1963–64
Charles Lynn Brown	1965
Hon. Voit Gilmore	1966–68
William H. Westphal	1968–70
C. C. Hope	1970–73

Orchestra Personnel in the First Concert (May 14, 1932)

VIOLINS

Alderman, Mrs. Jess, *Greensboro*

Edwards, Mrs. J. D., *Wilmington*

Foster, Miss Mildred, *Charlotte*

Hanaman, Miss Elizabeth, *Greensboro*

McCorkle, T. Smith, *Chapel Hill*

Sinclair, W. T., *Charlotte*

Thomas, James J., *Raleigh*

Blumenthal, Albert, *Winston-Salem*

Fidler, A. E., *High Point*

Frank, Miss Virginia, *High Point*

Kutschinski, C. D., *Winston-Salem*

MacPherson, D. A., *Chapel Hill*

Smith, Israel, *Charlotte*

Webb, Miss Susan, *Wilmington*

Wolslagel, Earl W., *Asheville*

VIOLAS

Giduz, Hugo, *Chapel Hill*

Johnson, Thor, *Winston-Salem*

Hartsook, Edward, *Greensboro*

Miller, Esta, *Charlotte*

'CELLOS

Bryant, Max, *Durham*

Greene, William S., *Charlotte*

Pier, Charles, *Southern Pines*

Fields, Dan, *Greensboro*

Hoffman, Elizabeth, *High Point*

Royster, Wilbur, *Raleigh*

BASSES

Alderman, Jess, *Greensboro*

Lawrence, George, *Chapel Hill*

Parrish, Henry, *Greensboro*

FLUTES

Rheaume, Ray, *Asheville*   Slocum, Earl, *Greensboro*

OBOES

Hazelman, Herbert, *Asheville*   Nanzetta, Leonard, *Greensboro*

CLARINETS

Glass, Charles, *Asheville*   Porter, Waldo, *Greensboro*

BASSOONS

King, Walter, *Greensboro*   Martin, Ruth, *Charlotte*

HORNS

Brietz, Raymond, Jr., *Winston-*   Gibbons, H. F., *Winston-Salem*
  Salem   White, Joseph, *Greensboro*
Schallert, Paul, *Winston-Salem*

TRUMPETS

Ahearn, E. J., *Greensboro*   Cousins, M. T., Jr., *Durham*
Smith, Robert C., *Charlotte*   Varnon, Miss Myrtle, *Greensboro*

TROMBONES

Lucas, Silas, *Wilson*   Mitchell, William, *Greensboro*
                 Simmons, Robert, *Greensboro*

TYMPANI AND DRUMS

McCall, Fred B., *Chapel Hill*

Senate Bill 248 (1943)

S. B. 248   Chapter 755

AN ACT TO PLACE THE NORTH CARO-
LINA SYMPHONY SOCIETY, INCOR-
PORATED, UNDER THE PATRONAGE
AND CONTROL OF THE STATE, AND
TO AUTHORIZE THE GOVERNOR
AND COUNCIL OF STATE TO MAKE
AN ALLOTMENT FROM THE CONTIN-
GENCY AND EMERGENCY FUND IN
AID THEREOF.

Preamble:
Service of N.C.
Symphony
Society.

WHEREAS, the North Carolina Symphony Society, Incorporated, is an organization of citizens of this State interested in making fine music available to the people of the State and promoting interest and appreciation of fine music by the citizenship of the State; and

Non-profit
organization.

WHEREAS, the said Society is a non-stock, non-profit organization organized by patriotic North Carolinians for the said purpose, and has functioned since one thousand nine hundred and thirty-two by giving two hundred concerts in twenty cities and communities; and

Purposes
educational.

WHEREAS, the plan and the purposes of the said organization are distinctly educational,

particular emphasis being made on increasing
the love and appreciation of music by the
children of the State, by giving free concerts
for the children; and

Patronage of
State desired.

WHEREAS, it is desired by the members of
said Society to place it under the patronage
and control of the State, to the end that its
permanency may be assured and that the
State may to some extent lend financial aid
necessary for the support thereof: Now,
therefore,

*The General Assembly of North Carolina do
enact:*

Membership of
Board of
Directors.

SECTION 1. That the governing body of the
North Carolina Symphony Society, Incorporated, shall be a board of directors consisting
of sixteen members, of which the Governor
of the State and the Superintendent of Public
Instruction shall be ex officio members, and
four other members shall be named by the
Governor. The remaining ten directors shall
be chosen by the members of the North
Carolina Symphony Society, Incorporated, in
such manner and at such times as that body
shall determine.

Terms of members
appointed by
Governor.

SEC. 2. That of the four members first
named by the Governor, two shall be appointed for terms of two years each and two
for terms of four years each, and subsequent
appointments shall be made for terms of four
years each.

Adoption of
by-laws.

SEC. 3. That the said board of directors, when organized under the terms of this Act, shall have authority to adopt bylaws for the Society and said bylaws shall thereafter be subject to change only by a three fifths vote of a quorum of said board of directors.

Annual audits
by State Auditor.

Reports to
General Assembly.

SEC. 4. That it shall be the duty of the State Auditor to make an annual audit of the accounts of the North Carolina Symphony Society, Incorporated, and make a report thereof to the General Assembly at each of its regular sessions, and the said Society shall be under the patronage and the control of the State.

Allocation from
Contingency and
Emergency Fund.

SEC. 5. That the Governor and Council of State are hereby authorized and empowered to allot a sum not exceeding two thousand dollars ($2,000.00) a year from the Contingency and Emergency Fund to aid in the carrying on of the activities of the said Society; that all expenditures made by the said Society shall be subject to the Executive Budget Act of North Carolina.

Conflicting laws
repealed.

SEC. 6. That all laws and clauses of laws in conflict with this Act are hereby repealed.

SEC. 7. That this Act shall be in full force and effect from and after its ratification.

Ratified this the 10th day of March, 1943.

Life Members, North Carolina Symphony Society[1]

Mrs. Katherine Pendleton
   Arrington
Edward B. Benjamin
Mrs. Athol C. Burnham
Mrs. Ceasar Cone
Stephen Emery
Paul Green

Mrs. George J. Jenks
Kay Kyser
Mrs. Roland McClamroch
Mrs. Joseph Hyde Pratt
Mrs. William Meade Prince
Mrs. Thomas Proctor
Mrs. Grace P. Woodman

[1]The cost of a life membership was $1,000.
This classification was later discontinued.

Memorial Memberships

President Harry F. Comer announced in 1945 that the first Memorial Membership to the N.C. Symphony Society was given to honor the memory of Col. Joseph Hyde Pratt.[1] By 1968, when Memorial Memberships were discontinued, there was a total of eighteen dedicatory memberships as indicated below:

JOSEPH HYDE PRATT—Given by his wife, Mrs. Joseph Hyde Pratt, Chapel Hill, and Dr. and Mrs. Joseph Hyde Pratt, Jr., Rochester, Minnesota.

BETTY BYRD GREEN—Given by her son, Paul Green of Chapel Hill.

FRANCES BADHAM BASON—Given by her daughter, Mrs. Athol C. Burnham, Chapel Hill.

LIEUTENANT MARSHALL McLANEY SHEPHERD—Given by his parents, Mr. and Mrs. J. G. Shepherd, Charlotte.

MARY LILY KENAN FLAGLER—Given by her sister, Mrs. Graham Kenan, Wilmington.

GEORGE HALEY—Given by James Street, Chapel Hill.

ERIC BERTHOLD SCHWARZ—Given by his parents, Dr. and Mrs. Berthold T. Schwarz, Montclair, New Jersey.

---

[1]At a meeting on Sept. 19, 1965, the Executive Committee of the Board of Trustees approved the establishment of a new Memorial Fund. The amount of the Memorial Membership was changed from $500 to $1,000 as of July 1967. These gifts honoring the memory of relatives or friends could be donated by an individual, a group of individuals, or an organization. A brief inscription was printed in the annual Tour Book, and at an appropriate concert the orchestra performed a special selection as a tribute to the person memorialized.

MABELLE BEATEY—Given by the Altrusa Club, Winston-Salem.

LIEUTENANT MARCUS VINCENT COURTNEY—Given by his parents, Mr. and Mrs. M. H. Courtney, Charlotte.

O. MAX GARDNER—Given by Mrs. O. Max Gardner and members of her family, from Shelby.

VANCE C. WEAVER—Given by appreciative people of Shelby and Cleveland County.

WILLIAM MEADE PRINCE—Given by his wife, the late Lillian Hughes Prince, Chapel Hill.

ELIZABETH LOTTE FRANZOS—Given by Mrs. Harmon L. Duncan and the late Harmon L. Duncan, Durham.

ALICE DAISY WARRINGTON—Given by her daughter-in-law, Mrs. Ralph Warrington, New Bern.

RUSSELL M. GRUMMAN—Given by his wife, Vida Seely Church Grumman.

HARMON L. DUNCAN—Given by his wife, Mrs. Harmon L. Duncan, Durham.

MRS. OLIVER HOKE SIMS of Nashville, Tenn.—Given by her daughter, Mrs. O. Meredith Shaw, New Bern.

MRS. EDWARD C. CURNEN—Given by her many and devoted friends.

Orchestra Personnel in the First Full-length Tour (1946)

VIOLIN
Perky, Mrs. Gregory
Poteet, Ewing
Barstow, Barbara
Rosenberger, Rachel
Gutheil, Crystal
Cohen, Sol
Berger, Ann
Moore, William
Bennett, George
Mantz, Theodora
Edwards, Mrs. Sam
Southwick, Richard
Schreiber, Nelson
Barbee, Samuel
Spiro, Margaret
Straus, Mrs. Erwin
McCulley, Edamay
Edwards, Virginia
Pagnato, Alfred
Merkley, Harold
Yost, Betty
Dawson, Mrs. Margaret
Butler, Mrs. Ray
Scheinberg, Harriet
Teeter, Mrs. Henry

VIOLA
Kutschinski, C. D.
Citron, Samuel
Guile, George
Brown, Louis
Slechta, Joseph
Bennett, Robert
Prunty, Phyllis
Evanoff, Thomas

VIOLONCELLO
Medlin, Charles
Adams, Shirley
Bullis, Helen
Greene, William
Heffernan, W. P.
Spencer, Clyde
Borden, Nadine
Scheinberg, Marion
Pappas, Mary

DOUBLE BASS
Luboff, A. G.
Andrews, Richard
Balmer, Wayne
Gaffney, Harris
Baughman, Isabel

PICCOLO
Crisman, Shirley

FLUTE
Burgess, John
Crisman, Shirley
Shaw, P. S.

OBOE
Storch, Laila
Morrow, Bernard

ENGLISH HORN
Storch, Laila

CLARINET
Sebren, Harbert
Barber, Raymond

BASSOON
Dawson, Robert
Curtin, Rosemary
Plaster, Richard
Moore, Mary Louise

FRENCH HORN
Beard, Richard
Hine, Mildred
Abbott, Kenneth
Rummel, R.
Crisp, Clay

TRUMPET
Blackford, Betty

Bourque, Irving
McDougle, Harold

TROMBONE
Merello, George
Wells, Max E.
Zam, Charles
Emde, J. C. M.

TUBA
Clark, Robert

TYMPANI
Spector, Stanley

PERCUSSION
Schinstine, William
McCall, F. B.
Williams, Edward

HARP
Perley, Marian

PIANO
Swalin, Maxine

LIBRARIAN
Barbee, Samuel

ORGAN
Cooper, Harry E.

Chairmen of the Symphony Ball (1961–71)

1961

Mrs. L. Richardson Preyer
Greensboro

Judge L. Richardson Preyer
Greensboro

1962

Mrs. William C. Friday
Chapel Hill

Mrs. James Kay Kyser
Chapel Hill

1963

Mrs. Howard Holderness
Greensboro

Mrs. Deryl Hart
Durham

1964

Mrs. Ralph B. Reeves, Jr.
Raleigh

Mr. John Belk
Charlotte

1965

Mrs. Roger Gant
Burlington

Mr. Lewis Holding
Raleigh

1966

Mrs. Nello Teer, Jr.
Durham

Mr. M. F. Browne
Raleigh

1967

Mrs. Voit Gilmore
Southern Pines

Mr. Shearon Harris
Raleigh

1968

Mrs. Earl N. Phillips
High Point

Mr. C. C. Cameron
Charlotte

1969

Mrs. W. Arthur Tripp
Greenville

Dr. Leo W. Jenkins
Greenville

1970

Mrs. Leslie N. Boney, Jr.
Wilmington

Mr. Louie E. Woodbury, Jr.
Wilmington

Mrs. C. C. Hope, Jr.
Charlotte

Mr. John D. Creadick
Asheville

1971

Mrs. Norris L. Hodgkins, Jr.
Durham

Mr. James M. Poyner
Raleigh

Assistant and Guest Conductors of the Symphony

ASSISTANT CONDUCTORS
Marion Rogers 1962–66
William Kirsche 1967–69
Jackson Parkhurst 1970–71
Thomas Conlin 1971–72
Alfred Heller 1971–72

GUEST CONDUCTORS
John Shenaut 1967
Valter Poole 1970–71

Index